All-in-One

BIBLE

FUN

Stories of Jesus
Elementary

ABINGDON PRESS
Nashville

All-in-One Bible Fun
Stories of Jesus
Elementary

ISBN 9781426707797

09 10 11 12 13 14 15 16 17 18 - 10 9 8 7 6 5 4 3 2 1

MANUFACTURED IN THE UNITED STATES OF AMERICA

All-in-One BIBLE FUN

Table of Contents

Bible Units in *Stories of Jesus*

Use these suggestions if you choose to organize the lessons in short-term units.

Jesus—Nativity and Childhood

Bible Story	Bible Verse
In the Stable	To you is born this day in the city of David a Savior, who is the Messiah, the Lord. (Luke 2:11)
By the Star's Light	The people who walked in darkness / have seen a great light. (Isaiah 9:2)
With the Elders	The Word became a human being and lived among us. (John 1:14, GNT, adapted)

Jesus—His Ministry

Bible Story	Bible Verse
At the River	And a voice came from heaven, "You are my Son, the Beloved." (Luke 3:22)
In the Desert	Worship the Lord Your God, / and serve only him. (Luke 4:8)
At the Synagogue	The Spirit of the Lord is upon me. (Luke 4:18)
By the Sea	Come with me, and I will teach you to catch people. (Matthew 4:19, GNT)

Jesus—Teachings

Bible Story	Bible Verse
On the Hillside	Listen to what you are taught. Be wise; do not neglect it. (Proverbs 8:33, GNT)
Through the Roof	Think of what Jesus went through. So do not let yourselves become discouraged and give up. (Hebrews 12:3, GNT, adapted)
With His Friends	The greatest love you can have for your friends is to give your life for them. (John 15:13, GNT)

Jesus—Death and Resurrection

Bible Story	Bible Verse
Out of the Tomb	For nothing will be impossible with God. (Luke 1:37)
On the Road	The Lord has risen indeed. (Luke 24:34)
With Us Always	And remember, I am with you always, to the end of the age. (Matthew 28:20)

All-in-One BIBLE FUN Supplies

(This is a comprehensive list of all the supplies needed if you choose to do all the activities, listed as they appear in this guide. It is your choice whether your group will do all the activities.)

- Bibles
- crayons, multi-cultural crayons
- balloons
- buttons, checkers, or packing peanuts
- watercolor and permanent felt-tip markers
- construction paper
- scissors
- masking tape and clear tape
- decorating supplies (dried coffee grounds, sand or sawdust, clay twigs, dried grass, pieces of fabric. and so forth)
- hay or raffia
- shallow bowls or dishes
- tempera paint, paint brushes
- plastic sandwich bags
- newspaper
- small white paper plates
- stapler, staples
- crepe paper streamers
- string, yarn, ribbon
- Epsom salts
- paper cups
- white glue
- cotton balls
- pastry brushes
- cardboard tubes
- saw, hammer, nails, wood, etc.
- books with pictures of Jesus
- plastic dishpan, iron, paper towels, plastic spoons
- paper punch
- index cards
- drinking straws
- corrugated cardboard sheets
- lunch-size paper bags, rubber bands

- aluminum foil
- drawing paper
- neon-colored printer paper
- scarfs/blindfolds
- shoeboxes
- envelopes
- large paper grocery bags
- unsharpened pencils
- pennies or metal washers
- blue fabric
- electric fan
- newsprint
- plastic ring soft drink holders
- art tissue
- sweatshirts, sweatpants, hats, scarfs, shoes
- flip flops
- round-headed clothespin or small plastic action figure
- cardboard boxes or trash cans
- ball
- sheet or blanket
- plain wrapping paper
- old greeting cards
- wax paper
- CD player and CD of Christian music
- clean-up supplies

All-in-One BIBLE FUN

Welcome to All-in-One Bible Fun

Have fun learning about the life of Jesus. Each lesson in this teacher guide is filled with games and activities that will make learning fun for you and your children. With just a few added supplies, everything you need to teach is included in Abingdon's *All-in-One Bible Fun*. Each lesson has a box with a picture of a cookie,

Jesus is the Messiah God promised to send.

that is repeated over and over again throughout the lesson. The cookie box states the Bible message in words your children will understand.

Use the following tips to help make *All-in-One Bible Fun* a success!

- Read through each lesson. Read the Bible passages.
- Memorize the Bible verse and the cookie box statement.
- Choose activities that fit your unique group of children and your time limitations. If time is limited, we recommend those activities noted in **boldface** on the chart page and by a *balloon* beside each activity.
- Practice telling the Bible story.
- Gather supplies you will use for the lesson.
- Learn the music included in each lesson. All the songs are written to familiar tunes.
- Arrange your room space to fit the lesson. Move tables and chairs so there is plenty of room for the children to move and to sit on the floor.
- Copy the Reproducible pages for the lesson.

balloon symbol

All-in-One Bible Fun

Stories of Jesus

Elementary

Also available from Abingdon Press

All-in-One Bible Fun
Stories of Jesus
Preschool

Writers/Editors: LeeDell Stickler, Daphna Flegal
Production Editors: Billie Brownell, Anna Raitt
Production and Design Manager: Marcia C'deBaca
Illustrator: Megan Jeffery
Cover photo: jupiterimages

Elementary

Each child in your class is a one-of-a-kind child of God. Each child has his or her own name, background, family situation, and set of experiences. It is important to remember and celebrate the uniqueness of each child. Yet these one-of-a-kind children of God have some common needs.

- All children need love.
- All children need a sense of self-worth.
- All children need to feel a sense of accomplishment.
- All children need to have a safe place to be and express their feelings.
- All children need to be surrounded by adults who love them.
- All children need to experience the love of God.

Younger elementary children (ages 6-10 years old) also have some common characteristics.

Their Bodies

- They are growing at different rates.
- They are energetic, restless, and have difficulty sitting still.
- They are developing fine motor skills.
- They want to participate rather than watch or listen.

Their Minds

- They are developing basic academic skills.
- They are eager to learn new things.
- They learn best by working imaginatively and creatively.
- They have little sense of time.
- They are concrete thinkers and cannot interpret symbols.
- They are developing an ability to reason and discuss.
- They like to have a part in planning their own activities.

Their Relationships

- They want to play with other children.
- They are sensitive to the feelings of others.
- They are shifting dependence from parents to teachers.
- They enjoy team activities but often dispute the rules.
- They imitate adults in attitudes and actions.

Their Hearts

- They are open to learning about God.
- They need caring adults who model Christian behaviors.
- They need to sing, move to, and say Bible verses.
- They need to hear simple Bible stories.
- They can talk with God easily if encouraged.
- They are asking questions about God.
- They can share food and money and make things for others.

All-in-One
BIBLE ELEMENTARY
FUN

In the Stable

Bible Verse

To you is born this day in the city of David a Savior,
who is the Messiah, the Lord.

Luke 2:11

Bible Story

Luke 2:1-20

Mary and Joseph had to travel to Bethlehem
to be counted for a census just prior to the
birth of their baby. Joseph was a descendent
of King David, so Bethlehem was the place
where they had to go. Bethlehem was
approximately 85 miles south of Nazareth,
the town where Joseph and Mary lived.

The tired couple arrived in Bethlehem after
their long journey to find that the large
number of pilgrims already there had filled
most of the available guest rooms. Mary and
Joseph were forced to seek shelter in a
caravansary, which served as an inn. Inns in
those days were likely to be dirty,
unfurnished, and poorly managed. Joseph
and Mary found themselves staying
overnight with the animals in a stable when
the inn had no more room. It was in the
stable that Jesus was born. The King of kings
might have been born in a stable but his
birth was announced from the heavens.
However, the ones to hear the good news

were a group of shepherds on a hillside
outside of town. These workers were also
the first to seek out the newborn Savior.
Awed by the angel's message, they
immediately left in search of the baby Jesus.
They told others, after seeing the baby, of the
marvelous event they had just witnessed.

Who would you choose to be the first to
hear the news of the greatest birth of the
century? Would you choose to have the
important announcement delivered to the
marginalized of society? Probably not.
Chances are you would have chosen the
most influential persons of your society. But
when God decided to send Jesus into the
world, Jesus came as an ordinary person.
He lived an ordinary life with ordinary
parents. Jesus could therefore identify with
the poor people of his day and with their
struggles. How appropriate that Jesus' life
story should begin in the humblest
fashion—in an animal shelter.

Jesus is the Savior God promised.

If time is limited, we recommend those activities that are noted in **boldface**. Depending on your time and the number of children, you may be able to include more activities.

ACTIVITY	TIME	SUPPLIES	
Christmas Creche	15 minutes	Reproducibles 1A and 1B, scissors, crayons or felt-tip markers, white glue, tape, decorating supplies such as dried coffee grounds, sand or sawdust, clay, twigs, dried grass, pieces of fabric, and so forth	**JOIN THE FUN**
Animal Arias	**10 minutes**	**blindfold**	
Who Are You?	5 minutes	None	**BIBLE STORY FUN**
Sing and Celebrate	5 minutes	None	
Bible Story: God's Own Son	**10 minutes**	**None**	
Story-Go-Round	5 minutes	index cards, felt-tip markers, ball	
Do-Wa-Ditty-Ditty	5 minutes	index cards, felt-tip markers in red and blue	**LIVE THE FUN**
Stable Prayers	**5 minutes**	**hay or raffia**	

11

Supplies

Reproducibles 1A and 1B, scissors, crayons or felt-tip markers, white glue, tape, decorating supplies such as dried coffee grounds, sand or sawdust, clay, twigs, dried grass, pieces of fabric. and so forth

Christmas Creche

Make a copy of the Nativity background **(Reproducibles 1A and 1B)** for each child or team of children in the class. Provide a box for the diorama that is about the same size as a shoe box. If you have a large class let children work together on the project. Smaller classes will enjoy making individual creches.

Welcome the children as they arrive. Get them started on their project(s). Show them how to cut apart the two background pieces and tape or glue them together to form a continuous background. Attach the background to the back of the box(es). Let the children add the figures of the holy family and the shepherds. Provide dried coffee grounds, sand, or sawdust for the stable floor(s). Let the children use their imaginations as to how to furnish their stable(s). Display the scenes during the season (*if you are doing this unit during the Christmas season*).

Supplies

blindfold

Animal Arias

Have the children be seated and form a circle. Blindfold one player to be "IT" and lead him or her to the center of the circle. IT will rotate in place with one arm outstretched. When IT stops, IT will ask the player to whom he or she is pointing to make a sound that baby Jesus might have heard as he slept in the stable.

IT must then identify the player from the sound the person makes. If IT is successful the player and IT change places. You might want to save this for later in the lesson if you have a class where children don't know one another.

Jesus is the Savior God promised.

12

Who Are You?

Supplies

None

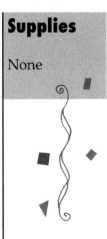

Have the children sit on the floor in a large circle.

Say: Today we are going to play a game of names. Names were important during Bible times. The angels, as we study the story of Christmas, were very insistent about the name that would be given to the child who would be born to Mary and Joseph. Names often identified peoples' status to others. Jesus, for example, would have been known as Jesus bar Joseph, which means Jesus, son of Joseph. But we know Jesus as Jesus, Son of God, Jesus as Messiah, Jesus as Savior, and Jesus as Prince of Peace.

Continue: Let's play a game of names. As we go around the circle each of you will give your name and some important fact about yourself. You can choose what this fact will be. It can be your favorite food, your favorite game, or your favorite color. I might say, for example, "My name is (*give your name*), and I like to teach Sunday school." Listen very carefully because I want to see how well each of you remembers.

When everyone has given his or her name, have all the class members stand up. Then select someone from the group. (Use volunteers at first to avoid embarrassing persons who might be unsure.) The person you select will try to name each of the other persons and identify his or her special fact. If the identification is correct that person will sit down. If not, the namer may have one hint. If the namer gets stuck a second time everyone will stand back up and another person will be chosen.

Sing and Celebrate

Supplies

None

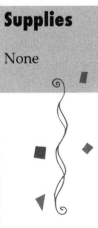

Sing together the song "The Kind Old Innkeeper" to the tune of "Old MacDonald." Let the children name different animals to include in the song.

The Kind Old Innkeeper
(Tune: "Old MacDonald")

The Kind Innkeeper had a stable,
On that starry night.
And in the stable he had a donkey,
On that starry night.
With a hee haw here, and hee haw there;
Here a hee, there a haw.
E'vrywhere a hee haw.
The Kind Innkeeper had a stable,
On that starry night.

The Kind Innkeeper had a stable,
On that starry night.
And in the stable he had a (*name animal*),
On that starry night.
With a (*animal sound*), and (*animal sound*) there;
Here a (*animal sound*), there a (*animal sound*).
E'vrywhere a (*animal sound*).
The Kind Innkeeper had a stable,
On that starry night.

Words: Daphna Flegal © 1997 Abingdon Press.

13

God's Own Son

by LeeDell Stickler

Teach the children the response to the story and the hand motions that go with it. The response is sung to the tune of "Little Cabin in the Woods."

Little stable in the town
(Make a tent overhead with your hands, fingertips touching.)
Bright starlight is shining down.
(Hold both hands up, fingers outstretched.
Wiggle fingers as you bring your arms down.)
Tiny baby, God's own Son
(Pretend to be rocking a baby.)
Jesus is the One.
(Touch the palm of your left hand with the middle finger of your right hand;
touch the palm of your right hand with the middle finger of your left hand.
Then hold up the index finger of your right hand, indicating the number 1.)

Have the children practice the signs and the words until they feel comfortable with the refrain.

God looked down at the earth. "I can't believe it! Even with all the laws I have given them, they still haven't gotten it right. I've even sent my prophets, but the people ignore them. Nothing seems to make a difference. There's only one thing left to do. I'll send my Son. He'll teach them what they need to know. He'll show them how to love one another and care for one another. He'll set an example for them."

Sing refrain with motions.

"First I have to choose just the right family to care for my Son. I don't want the family to be rich and powerful because then my Son will not know what it means to be just an ordinary boy. I want my Son grow up like any normal boy and to learn to make his living, just like the rest must do."

Sing refrain with motions.

So God looked around and found the perfect place and the perfect family. God chose a young girl from the village of Nazareth. Her

14

name was Mary. She was engaged to marry Joseph, the carpenter in the village. And God said, "Mary will be a good mother for my Son. Joseph will watch out for her and for the child. They are just right."

Sing refrain with motions.

The emperor Augustus decreed that all men had to return to their hometowns to be counted for a census. Even though it was very close to the time for her baby to be born, Mary and Joseph made the trip to Bethlehem. But when they got there the town was so crowded that there were no rooms. All that was left was a little stable filled with the animals of travelers. That is just where God's Son was born, in a tiny stable with only the animals to keep watch.

Sing refrain with motions.

God called the angels together. "I want everyone to know about this special baby. Go, tell the people that their Savior has been born."

Sing refrain with motions.

So the angels looked all about. They wanted to find someone who would be excited about this good news. The rich and the powerful were much too busy to take time to celebrate the birth of a poor baby. So the angels found a group of shepherds who were out on the hillside. And they began to sing the good news of the Savior's birth to them.

Sing refrain with motions.

At first the shepherds were frightened. But then they looked at one another and began to wonder why God had chosen them to hear the wonderful news. They were excited and decided to find the child that the angels had told them about.

Sing refrain with motions.

BIBLE STORY FUN

Supplies

index cards, felt-tip markers, ball

Story-Go-Round

Say: Today we heard the story of the birth of God's Son Jesus. We hear this story every year at Christmas. We read the story from the Bible. It's a wonderful story to tell over and over again because we love Jesus and know how special he is. But did you ever really think about what it was like to be born in a stable? Close your eyes and imagine what it was like to be in that stable.

Ask: Was it cold or warm in the stable? Was it clean or dirty? How did the stable smell? How did the hay feel? What animals might have been there?

Let the children name all the animals they can think of that might have been in the stable the night that Jesus was born. Write each animal's name down on an index card. Some possible animals might be: sheep, cow, ox, donkey, camel, goat, cat, mouse, spider, flea, or dove. Shuffle the index cards.

Ask: If you had been one of the animals in the stable the night Jesus was born, what would you have seen or thought or done?

Say: I am going to roll the ball to someone in the group. Come draw a card with an animal's name on it. Pretend you are that animal and were present that night. Tell us what you saw.

Continue around the circle until each of the children has had a chance to share the story from the points of view of the animals.

Ask: Where might Jesus have been born if he were born today? Would it be in a hospital? or in a house? Who might be watching?

Say: God didn't send God's Son to enjoy the fine life. God sent Jesus to be raised in the home of ordinary people—people who worked hard for a living. God wanted Jesus to identify with the people he had come to save.

 Jesus is the Savior God promised.

16

Supplies

index cards, felt-tip markers in red and blue

Do-Wa-Ditty-Ditty

Write the Bible verse on two sets of index cards in this manner: "To you is born," "this day," "in the city of David," "a Savior," "who is the Messiah, the Lord." Make a red set and a blue set with colored markers.

Read the Bible verse with the children several times. Then hand out the cards. *(If you have more than twelve children, divide the verse a little differently. If you have fewer than twelve children, just have one set of cards; don't play it as a team game.)*

Say: I am going to begin saying the Bible verse. I will leave out some words. Instead of the words, I'm going to say, "Do-wa-ditty-ditty." As soon as the person who is holding the missing phrase recognizes the phrase, that person will stand up and read that phrase.

The team that gets the phrase first receives a point if you are playing this game as a team game.

Stable Prayers

Supplies

hay or raffia

Have the children come to the floor and sit in a circle. Show the children the hay or raffia.

Say: Jesus was born in a stable for animals. His bed was a manger, the animal's feeding box. Let's pass this small bit of hay around the circle. Hold the hay for just a moment and think about how God's Son was born in a stable.

Have them bow their heads and pray after all the children have held the hay.

Pray: Dear God, we thank you for Jesus, the one you sent to be our Savior. Amen.

> **Jesus is the Savior God promised.**

17

REPRODUCIBLE 1A

ALL-IN-ONE BIBLE FUN

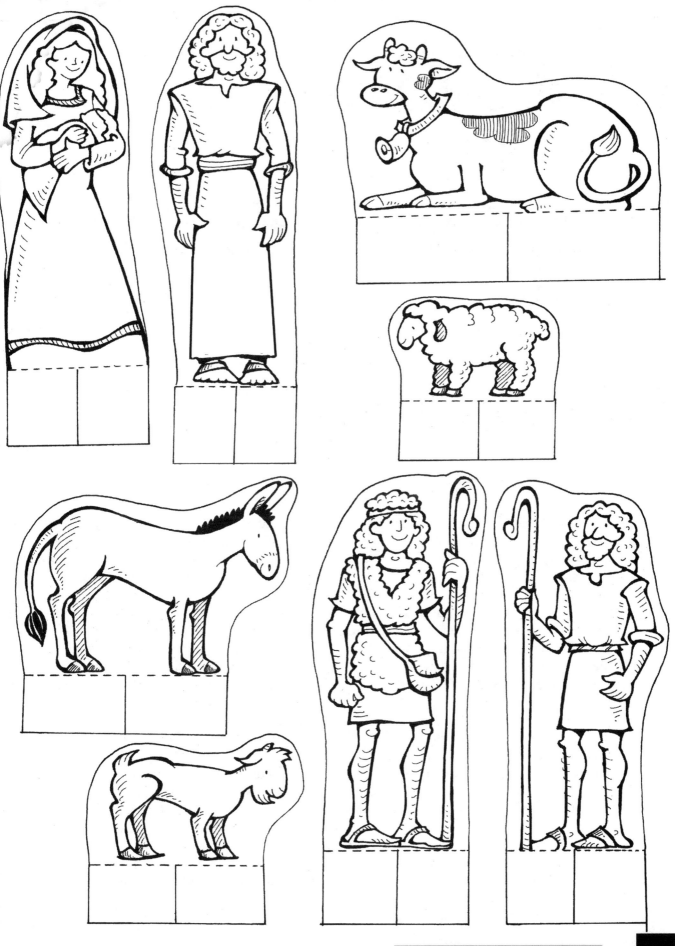

By the Star's Light

Bible Verse

The people who walked in darkness
have seen a great light.

Isaiah 9:2

Bible Story

Matthew 2:1-12

The story of the star and the scholars who traveled afar can be found in the Book of Matthew. Matthew wanted his readers to understand that these visitors came from outside the realm of Jewish society. Many scholars in fact believe that these wise men were astrologers, or Median priests. Because they had seen the sign and had chosen to follow it, Jesus was obviously not just the Messiah of the Jews, but the Savior for all people everywhere.

Much tradition has grown up around the story of the magi. The Scriptures never actually tell us that there were three. We simply assume this because there were three gifts named in the Bible. The gifts themselves hold great significance. Gold, frankincense, and myrrh are hardly gifts to bestow upon a baby boy. These are gifts much more appropriate to royalty. It is this presentation of gifts to the Christ child that has been the inspiration for gift-giving at Christmas.

The wise men did not arrive until Jesus was roughly two years old. We calculate this because King Herod had ordered the death of all male Jewish children up to two years old, hoping to rid himself of the threat of a new king. Jesus' family had long since abandoned the stable where Jesus was born and were staying in a house in the city. (Why they should still be in Bethlehem after two years is still a mystery.) How surprised Mary and Joseph must have been when the strange men arrived, knelt down, and worshiped their child—hardly a normal reaction to seeing a young child. Fortunately, the magi were able to thwart King Herod's plans, with God's help. Instead of reporting back to Herod, the scholars returned to their homeland by a different route, and they never told the king where he could find Jesus. This story and the symbols and traditions that come from this story are all parts of our Christmas traditions.

Jesus is the Savior God sent to all people everywhere.

If time is limited, we recommend those activities that are noted in **boldface**. Depending on your time and the number of children, you may be able to include more activities.

ACTIVITY	TIME	SUPPLIES
What the Magi Saw	**5 minutes**	Reproducible 2A, crayons or markers
Secret Signs	5 minutes	None
Star Crowns	15 minutes	Reproducible 2B, scissors, neon-colored printer paper; stapler and staples or glue, tape
Sing and Celebrate	5 minutes	None
Bible Story: Follow That Star!	**10 minutes**	**star crowns (Reproducible 2B)**
All That Glitters	10 minutes	Epsom salts; water; construction paper (black, dark blue, dark red, dark green); newspaper; small paper cups; pastry brushes, foam paintbrush, or cotton balls; crayons; optional: hair dryer or small electric fan
Royal Ruckus	5 minutes	balloon, permanent marker
Star Prayers	**5 minutes**	**balloon with star from Royal Ruckus, or one star crown (Reproducible 2B)**

What the Magi Saw

Supplies

Reproducible 2A, crayons or markers

Make a copy of the coloring puzzle (**Reproducible 2A**) for each child in your group.

Say: **One of my favorite stories at Christmas has always been the story of the magi, or wise men, who came to visit Jesus.**

Ask: **How did they know that a new king had been born? What was the special sign?**

Have the children color the puzzle and discover the secret sign.

> **Jesus is the Savior God sent to all people everywhere.**

Secret Signs

Supplies

None

Bring the children together. Have them be seated in their chairs and form a circle. (If you have limited space, this can be done around a table where the chairs have been pushed back.)

Say: **We are going to play a game of secret signs. When I make the secret signs everyone will do what the sign tells you to do. Everyone will move over one chair to the right when I pull my earlobe.** (*Pull your earlobe and let everyone move one chair to the right.*) **Everyone will move over one chair to the left when I touch my nose.** (*Touch your nose and let everyone shift one chair to the left.*) **Everyone will stand up when I scratch my chin.** (*Scratch your chin and let everyone stand up.*) **Is everyone ready?** (*You may want to practice one more time, and mix the signs up to get the children's attention.*)

Talk with the children about their experiences of the past week. Talk about their pets and their families. During the conversation, very subtly make the secret signs. Keep everyone moving. Quit after a few minutes.

Say: **In today's Bible story some people saw a secret sign. The sign told them what had happened and what they should do. The sign was the symbol that told them a new king had been born, and they went to find the king.**

Star Crowns

Supplies

Reproducible 2B, scissors, neon-colored printer paper, stapler and staples or glue, tape

Make a copy of the crown base (**Reproducible 2B**) for each child in the group. (If possible, run the photocopies on the neon-colored paper.) Cut the neon-colored printer paper into two-inch by eleven-inch strips. Each child will need approximately eight strips. (Children with smaller heads may need fewer strips.)

Have the children color and cut out the crown base. (For children with smaller heads, you may only need two strips and a portion of the third strip. Adjust after the coloring has been done.) Attach the strips to form one continuous star band.

Have the children choose eight strips of any color. Hold the ends of the strips together and staple (or glue), forming a large loop. (If you have a large class and only one stapler, then stapling the loops may be impractical. But stapling will speed the process.)

Fit the crown base to each child's head, and mark with a pencil so that there is only an overlap of about two inches. Mark the overlap line on the back of the band. Trim any excess from the band.

Place the crown base face-down on the table. Line the loops up side-by-side along the base, the stapled edges on the inside of the band, and the loops extending above the band. Staple or tape the loops in place. Staple or tape the ends of the band together to form the crown.

Let the children wear their crowns as they participate in the Bible story activity.

Sing and Celebrate

Supplies

None

Sing together the song "Shining Star" to the tune of "This Old Man." Let the children name different animals to include in the song.

Shining Star
(Tune: "This Old Man")

Shining star, shining star,
Shine to show us where you are.
Shine your light on little Bethlehem,
Guide the path of the wise men.

Words: Daphna Flegal © 2001 Abingdon Press.

Follow That Star!

by LeeDell Stickler

> **Ask: When you hear about the wise men who came to visit Jesus, what do you think of?** *(Let the children share their suggestions.)* **How many do you think there were?** *(Let the children state that there were three.)*
>
> Then have the children read Matthew 2:1-12. Read the passage for the children if they are not confident readers.
>
> **Say: Nowhere in the Bible text does it say there were three wise men. We assume there were three because of the three gifts they brought—gold, frankincense, and myrrh. But we really don't know. I wonder what would have happened if there had been more than three wise men—maybe the same number of them as there are children in this class?**
>
> Make a copy of the story for the children. Color-code each part. Give the numbered parts in order to the children in the line. Let the children have more parts if you have fewer than twelve. Have the children get in a line as if in a camel caravan. Have each place one hand on the shoulder of the person in front of her or him. Let them alternately bob up and down as though riding a camel as they walk around the room.

Wise Man #1: My backside hurts. When are we going to get there?

Wise Man #2: I sure wish we had a map. Following a star isn't easy. Are we lost?

Wise Man #3: Are you very sure this star is the one? It's big and bright, but is it the one?

Wise Man #4: Who would have thought the desert could be so cold at night? Do you think we should stop and get directions?

Wise Man #5: Do you think there's an oasis just up the way? I'm thirsty.

Wise Man #6: Who's got the gifts? Did someone remember the gifts?

Wise Man #7: I've got the gifts!! What do you think I've been sitting on for the past two years?

Wise Man #8: I sure hope the new king likes the gifts. I picked them out myself.

Wise Man #9: You did not! The whole group decided what to get—gifts fit for a king.

Wise Man #10: Well, I wonder what a baby is going to do with a bottle of frankincense.

Wise Man #11: Are we almost there yet? I need a bath and want to stretch my legs.

Wise Man #12: That city we just passed was pretty big. Don't you think a new king would live there if he had a choice?

Wise Man #1: You know, I don't trust King Herod. He's got shifty eyes.

Wise Man #2: When he told us he wanted to come to worship the child, his eye twitched. He was lying.

Wise Man #3: I think he wants to get rid of the child. But first we have to find him. Are you sure we're not lost?

Wise Man #4: Hey, does it look like the star has stopped moving to you?

Wise Man #5: Sure looks like it to me. But where are we?

Wise Man #6: In the middle of nowhere—the map says the town is called Bethlehem.

Wise Man #7: It looks too small to have a decent place to eat.

Wise Man #8: Wherever we are, the star is shining down on that house over there.

Wise Man #9: Shall we knock on the door? Would that be OK?

Wise Man #10: I didn't come all this way to turn around and leave. Go on. Knock.

Wise Man #11: At least if it's not the right house the people there can give us directions.

Wise Man #12: *(Knocks on door.)* We are wise men who have come a long way looking for a king. Is there one inside?

(All Wise Men kneel and hold up their hands as though presenting the child their gifts.)

Stories of Jesus - Elementary

Supplies

Epsom salts; water; construction paper (black, dark blue, dark red, dark green); newspaper; small paper cups; pastry brushes, foam paintbrush, or cotton balls; crayons; optional: hair dryer or small electric fan)

All That Glitters

Say: The star for Christians has come to represent the birth of baby Jesus and the visit from the magi. The people who heard this story about Jesus knew that God sent Jesus to everyone, not just to the Jewish people. This was because the magi were from a foreign country and probably were not Jewish. God sent Jesus to be the Savior of all people everywhere. Our Bible verse for today says that the people who had been living in darkness had seen a great light. Jesus was and is that light. But the most important thing of all is that Jesus is our Savior.

Give each child a piece of dark construction paper (black, dark blue, dark red, or dark green). Have them draw stars either with a pencil or create a template and let them trace the stars. Color in each of the stars with a light-colored crayon. Remind the children to color hard so that the crayon will cover all the paper in the star design.

Have the children write with a light crayon: "Jesus is the light." Remind them to bear down so that the crayon markings are thick. Recall with the children the fact that the wise men or magi watched the sky for signs. The new star was a special sign.

Mix equal parts of Epsom salts and water in a cup or small bowl. Stir until the mixture dissolves. Cover the tables with newspaper. Then let the children take a pastry brush, foam paintbrush, or cotton ball and dip it into the mixture. Rub the mixture over the picture.

Allow the pictures to dry. You might want to use a hair dryer or small electric fan to speed up the drying process if the children want to take the pictures home today. Anchor the papers before blowing, however. Watch the salt crystals appear.

> **Jesus is the Savior God sent to all people everywhere.**

Royal Ruckus

Supplies

balloon, permanent marker

Blow up and tie a balloon. Use the permanent marker to draw a star on the balloon.

Have the children stand in a circle and hold hands. Show the children the balloon. Point out the star.

Say: The star was a sign that the new king had been born. The magi saw the star and set out in search of the new king. God's people had been waiting for a long time for the Savior, the Messiah. God didn't send Jesus just to the Hebrews—God sent Jesus to everyone. Let's see if all of us, together, can keep that star shining.

Toss the balloon into the air. Players will attempt to keep the balloon from hitting the ground by using any parts of their bodies that may be necessary. The round will end when the balloon touches the ground or two players disconnect their hands.

Say the Bible verse together when the game is over: **"The people who walked in darkness have seen a great light."**

Star Prayers

Supplies

balloon with star from Royal Ruckus, or one star crown (Reproducible 2B)

Have the children come to the floor and sit in a circle. Show the children the balloon with the star or one of the star crowns.

Say: In today's story the star played a very important part. Today I want you to pass this star balloon (or star crown) around our circle. As you hold it, remember the long journey the wise men took to find the new king. They only had the sign of the star and the star's light to guide them. Then think about how Jesus brings light to your life.

Pass the star balloon or star crown around the circle. When the star makes its way all around the circle, have the children bow their heads.

Pray: Dear God, we thank you for Jesus, whom you sent to be the Savior of not just one small group of people, but of all people everywhere. Amen.

> ## Jesus is the Savior God sent to all people everywhere.

What did the wise men see?

Color all the spaces marked with a • black.
Color all the spaces marked with a + gray.

For we observed his _____ at its rising.

REPRODUCIBLE 2A

ALL-IN-ONE BIBLE FUN

With the Elders

Bible Verse

The Word became a human being and lived among us.

John 1:14, GNT, adapted

Bible Story

Luke 2:39-52

These verses in the Book of Luke are the only references to Jesus between the time of his infancy and the time that he started his ministry. What do they tell us about Jesus?

We learn from this story that Mary and Joseph were devout Jews, so we can assume that Jesus received the normal Jewish upbringing for a boy in Bible times. Jesus would have attended the synagogue and learned the Scriptures of the Old Testament. Three times every year he would have gone with his family (or at least his father) to the annual festivals prescribed for male Israelites. (Women were not required to attend, but frequently did.) The Passover celebration was particularly important. Jesus would have attended these festivals many times before he was twelve.

When Jesus was found in the Temple he was "sitting among the teachers listening to them and asking them questions." In one of

the halls of the Temple's outer courts the Rabbis used question, answer, and discussion to teach. However, at this young age, Jesus was unprepared to begin his ministry. So, being obedient to his earthly parents, he returned home where he "grew and became strong, filled with wisdom; and the favor of God was upon him."

Boys and girls enjoy hearing stories about children who lived in other times and in other places. It's interesting to compare how they did things with how we do things. Children wonder what Jesus was like as a child, a boy, and a teenager. Because the Bible doesn't spend much time on these times in Jesus' life, we have to piece together much of what we know from what we have learned about life in Bible times. God sent his Son Jesus to grow up as a boy in a typical family of that time. Jesus was not royalty. Jesus was not privileged. Jesus was just like the children you teach.

As Jesus grew he learned more about God's plan for his life.

If time is limited, we recommend those activities that are noted in **boldface**. Depending on your time and the number of children, you may be able to include more activities.

ACTIVITY	TIME	SUPPLIES	
Find the Missing Boy	**5 minutes**	**Reproducible 3A, pencils, crayons**	JOIN THE FUN
Discover the Plan	10 minutes	Reproducible 3B; construction paper; buttons, checkers, or packing peanuts	
School Days	10 minutes	Bible; paper; pencil or felt-tip marker; saw, hammer; nails, pieces of wood, sandpaper	BIBLE STORY FUN
Bible Story: Talking With the Elders	**10 minutes**	**None**	
Where Is Jesus?	10 minutes	round-headed clothespin and felt-tip marker or small plastic action figure	
Sing and Celebrate	5 minutes	None	
Picture Perfect	5 minutes	drawing paper; felt-tip markers, crayons (option: multicultural crayons); map; books or posters with pictures of Jesus	LIVE THE FUN
Growing Up Prayers	**5 minutes**	**figure used in "Where is Jesus?"**	

Find the Missing Boy

Reproducible 3A, pencils, crayons

Make a copy of the maze **(Reproducible 3A)** for each child in your group. Greet the children as they come in.

Ask: Do you ever wonder what Jesus was like as a boy? What games did he like to play? What were his friends like? Did he know what God had planned for him?

Say: The Bible doesn't tell us much about Jesus during that time of his life. In fact there is only one story we have. It tells about a time when he was about twelve years old, a special time in the life for a Jewish boy. At this time Jesus was beginning to learn about God's plan for his life.

Invite the children to solve the maze.

> **As Jesus grew he learned more about God's plan for his life.**

Discover the Plan

Supplies

Reproducible 3B; construction paper; buttons, checkers, or packing peanuts

Make a copy of the gameboard **(Reproducible 3B)** for each child. Give each player ten items (buttons, checkers, or packing peanuts). Have the children tear the construction paper into thumb-sized bits as markers. Divide the children into pairs. Have the pairs sit at a table facing each other, the gameboard facing them. Place a book between the two gameboards so that the children cannot see the opposing board. The object of this game is discover the opponent's plan (or arrangement). Each player has one minute to arrange all ten items on his or her gameboard. The items can be anywhere on the board, but each item must be touching the square of another item, horizontally, vertically, or diagonally.

The first player will call out a number when everyone is ready. If his or her opponent has an item on that square, the player will mark it with a piece of construction paper and try again. The opponent will say, "No way!" if the square is vacant, and the play will pass to the second player. At the end of the game the player with the most markers is the winner.

Say: You began to see the pattern and could earn points the longer you played. I wonder if that's what it was like for Jesus as he began to grow and learn about God's plan for his life.

School Days

Supplies

Bible; paper; pencil or felt-tip marker; saw, hammer; nails, pieces of wood, sandpaper

Bring the children together in a circle on the floor.

Say: Jesus was born. Shepherds came to the stable. Wise men brought gifts to the baby. Mary and Joseph fled to Egypt. But the Bible doesn't tell us what will happen next until ten more years have passed in Jesus' life. We can take what we know about life in Bible times and fill in some details. Joseph would have reopened his carpentry shop. Mary would have stayed at home and cared for the house and the children. The boy Jesus would have helped around the house. When he became five, Jesus would have gone to school at the synagogue. This school was called "a house of the book" where he learned scripture and learned to read and write Hebrew.

One at a time form each of the letters here and let the children duplicate them on their own pieces of paper. Then practice saying the letters out loud. Read John 1:14 from the Bible. Then read it again and let the children repeat the verse. Ask the children to discuss what the verse means. School in Bible times would have been like this.

Say: At age ten a boy would go on to a higher level of school called "the house of learning." There he would learn the written and oral laws of the Hebrew people. When boys were not in school, they would learn crafts or trades. Jesus would have helped Joseph in the carpentry shop.

Give the children an opportunity to experiment with the various tools and lumber. Caution them to be careful so they do not injure themselves or others.

Say: Girls did not go to school, but learned what they needed to know from their mothers. They learned to prepare the food in the special ways required by their religion. They learned to decorate their homes for the sabbath and set the table for special holy days. Girls also learned to spin, weave, and take care of the sick. Many learned to sing, dance, or play musical instruments.

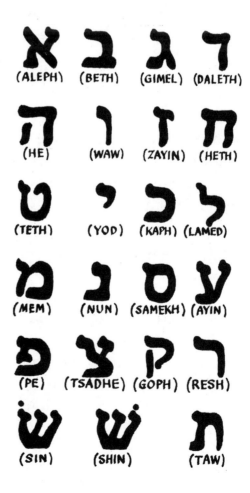

א (ALEPH)	ב (BETH)	ג (GIMEL)	ד (DALETH)
ה (HE)	ו (WAW)	ז (ZAYIN)	ח (HETH)
ט (TETH)	י (YOD)	כ (KAPH)	ל (LAMED)
מ (MEM)	נ (NUN)	ס (SAMEKH)	ע (AYIN)
פ (PE)	צ (TSADHE)	ק (GOPH)	ר (RESH)
שׂ (SIN)	שׁ (SHIN)	ת (TAW)	

Talking With the Elders

by LeeDell Stickler

Say: Jesus was raised in a small town called Nazareth. Even though it was small, it was located on a major trade route, so certainly Jesus would have learned about what was happening in other parts of the country. But how excited Jesus must have been when it was his turn to go to Jerusalem for the Passover and be admitted to the Temple as a man! There he would get to meet and talk with the religious authorities of the day. Certainly he had many questions to ask them. But Jesus lost track of time and circumstance. You have heard the story before. Do you ever wonder why his family didn't miss him sooner? How could they have traveled for three days before they knew he was gone? There were many things going on that week. Let's hear from some of the people involved and see what was happening.

Tell this story using these characters: Mary, Joseph, Brother James, Cousin John, an Elder, and Jesus. In the story there is a section labeled "All." At this point the entire class will stand up, lift their shoulders, hold up both hands, palms up, and question: **Where is Jesus?** Make a copy of the story. Highlight each child's part.

Mary

I know he was with us when we got here. But so many people come to Jerusalem for the Passover. Our whole village came to celebrate. I just thought Jesus was with his cousins or our neighbors. But I know I haven't seen him since we started for home.

All: Where is Jesus?

Joseph

This was supposed to be a special Passover for Jesus. He is twelve. This year he could leave his mother and the rest of the women and children and come to where the men worshiped. According to our faith, Jesus is now a man. So when I didn't see him I didn't worry too much. I just thought he forgot and was with his mother. But now I know he isn't here.

All: Where is Jesus?

Brother James
Everything was so exciting. Jesus enjoyed being the older brother when there were so many people around. He helped me find my way through the marketplace. He knew where all the best places were to get food. But he didn't leave with us when Mother and the rest did. I just thought he was with our father.

All: Where is Jesus?

Cousin John
The last time I saw Jesus he was in the outer court with me. He heard some of the elders talking about a Scripture. This got his attention. So he sat down to listen. After a while I got bored, so I left him there. Maybe I shouldn't have. I haven't seen him since.

All: Where is Jesus?

Elder of the Synagogue
I saw a boy who matched his description at the Temple. He was in the Court of the Gentiles sitting at the feet of some of the teachers. He was talking about the Scriptures. He asked so many questions. And what questions they were! He showed great understanding for a boy his age. He really made you think about what the Scriptures mean. But I had things to do in other parts of the city. I couldn't listen for long. When I left the boy and the other elders were still sitting there talking.

All: Where is Jesus?

Jesus
What I can't understand is why there is such a fuss. I wasn't lost. Why should they even ask the question? Don't they know that if I would be anywhere I would be in God's house? This is where I've been the whole time. What an exciting time—just to talk to the elders about the Scriptures and what it means! I think they were surprised at all I knew.

Supplies

round-headed clothespin and felt-tip marker or small plastic action figure

Where Is Jesus?

If you use a clothespin, draw a face on the clothespin with the marker.

Bring the children together in a circle in the center of the room. Select one child to come to the center and be "IT." Then have the rest of the class stand shoulder to shoulder facing inside, with their hands behind their backs.

Say: Let's play a game. In this game the person in the center is going to be Mary or Joseph. Jesus is missing and it is up to the person in the center to try to find out just where Jesus is. This clothespin or figure will represent the boy Jesus as he makes his way around Jerusalem during Passover. Let's see if IT can discover where he is.

Place the clothespin or figure in a child's hand and let the children pass it around behind their backs. When IT calls out "Stop!" then movement stops. IT can make one guess as to who IT thinks has the figure. IT may start and stop the movement three times and make three guesses. If IT cannot find the figure in three guesses, then the last person to have the figure gets to come to the center and be IT. Encourage the children who are standing in the circle to make deceptive movements that might trick IT into thinking that they are the ones passing the figure. IT will have to watch very carefully. Make sure the children are standing very close together.

Play until all the children have had the opportunity to be IT.

Say: The Bible doesn't tell us much about Jesus and what he was like as a child or a boy or even as a young man. We will not hear another story about Jesus until he is about thirty-three years old.

Ask: What did he do during those twenty-two years? What kind of a person was he? Who were his friends?

Sing and Celebrate

Supplies

None

Sing together the song "In the Temple Courts" to the tune of "The Paw Paw Patch."

In the Temple Courts
(Tune: "The Paw Paw Patch")

Where, oh where is our son Jesus?
Where, oh where is our son Jesus?
Where, oh where is our son Jesus?
We've been looking for him everywhere.

Here oh here, is your son Jesus.
Here oh here, is your son Jesus.
Here oh here, is your son Jesus.
He is sitting in the Temple courts.

Picture Perfect

Draw a circle in the center of a piece of drawing paper to represent a face. Have the children sit where they can easily see the paper.

Ask: What word in our Bible verse for today stands for Jesus? *(Read the Bible verse aloud.)* **What does this Bible verse tell us?** *(God sent Jesus to be a human being to live among us.)*

Say: We know a great deal about what Jesus said and did, but we really don't know what he looked like. Artists throughout history have drawn pictures of what they think Jesus looked like. But they usually made Jesus look a great deal like themselves. *(Share the pictures.)*

Say: Jesus lived in a part of the world that we call the Middle East. *(Locate Israel and Palestine on the map.)* **Because he lived there Jesus probably would have looked a certain way—dark skin, dark brown or black hair, and dark eyes.** *(Let the children choose a color crayon for the skin tone and color the face. Then add dark eyes and hair.)* **His hair would have probably been longish, and maybe even curly.** *(Let the children decide if the hair should be straight or curly. Then have them draw in the hair.)*

Ask: But what else would Jesus have been like? You can't always judge persons by the way they look. What are some words that you think would describe Jesus as he was living among the people?

Supplies

drawing paper, felt-tip markers, crayons (option: multi-cultural crayons), map, books or posters with pictures of Jesus

Growing Up Prayers

Have the children come to the floor and sit in a circle. Show the children the figure you used to represent Jesus in "Where Is Jesus?"

Say: In many ways Jesus grew up just like you. Today as we pass this figure around the circle, I want you to think what it might have been like to be Jesus. Think about all the things he might have done as a boy that you might do yourself.

Have the children join hands and form a prayer circle after the figure has gone all the way around the circle.

Pray: Dear God, we thank you for Jesus who was like us in so many ways. Help us to discover your plan for our lives just as Jesus discovered your plan for his life. Amen.

Supplies

figure used in "Where is Jesus?"

37

Help Mary and Joseph find their lost son.

Start →

Finish →

For we observed his _____ at its rising.

REPRODUCIBLE 3A

ALL-IN-ONE BIBLE FUN

5	10	15	20
4	9	14	19
3	8	13	18
2	7	12	17
1	6	11	16

Stories of Jesus - Elementary

All-in-One BIBLE ELEMENTARY FUN

At the River

Bible Verse

And a voice came from heaven, "You are my Son, the Beloved."

Luke 3:22

Bible Story

Luke 3:15-23

John, the son of Elizabeth and Zechariah, was a cousin of Jesus and grew up to be a preacher. God's plan was that he be the one to prepare the people for the coming of the kingdom of God. So John found himself in the wilderness, on the banks of the Jordan River, preaching, "Repent and be saved!" Then he would baptize the followers as a sign of this repentance.

Baptism did not start with John. It had long been practiced by Jews as a rite of religious purification to receive new converts into the Jewish faith. Gentiles wanting to convert to Judaism were baptized to cleanse themselves of non-Jewish beliefs and practices. However, the baptism John practiced was different. It was a rite of repentance so that sins could be forgiven. Baptism was (and is) an outward sign of an inward change. The ritual of baptism also marks a person as a member of the family of God.

Many persons have asked this question over the years: "Why did Jesus seek baptism from John?" Jesus had not led a sinful life that we are aware of up to this point. Perhaps it was Jesus' way of signifying the change of direction in his life. This action signaled that Jesus was ready to take on the mantle of his ministry. And when Jesus emerged from the water, a sign was given that identified Jesus as the true son of God.

The story of the baptism in Matthew 3:13-15 indicates that Jesus endorsed John's ministry. His baptism was meant to show all people an act of obedience to God's will. This would be consistent with Jesus' whole ministry—it showed people what obedience to God meant through both words and actions. Baptism is a special sacrament of the church, a recognition that God owns us. We belong to God.

Jesus is God's Son, the promised Savior.

If time is limited, we recommend those activities that are noted in **boldface**. Depending on your time and the number of children, you may be able to include more activities.

ACTIVITY	TIME	SUPPLIES	
What's Missing?	5 minutes	Reproducible 4A, crayons or felt-tip markers	JOIN THE FUN
Art Effects	**10 minutes**	**Reproducible 4B, watercolor felt-tip markers, plastic dish pan, newspaper, an iron, paper towels, cotton swabs, plastic spoons or eyedroppers**	JOIN THE FUN
Are You the One?	5 minutes	one small object such as an eraser, paper clip, or plastic block	BIBLE STORY FUN
Bible Story: John the Baptist Rap	**10 minutes**	**None**	BIBLE STORY FUN
Glide On	10 minutes	Reproducible 4B, scissors, paper clip, masking tape	BIBLE STORY FUN
Sing and Celebrate	5 minutes	None	BIBLE STORY FUN
Spread the Word	10 minutes	dove glider (Reproducible 4B)	LIVE THE FUN
Dove Prayers	**5 minutes**	**dove glider (Reproducible 4B)**	LIVE THE FUN

Supplies

Reproducible 4A, crayons or felt-tip markers

What's Missing?

Make a copy of the arrival activity **(Reproducible 4A)** for each child in the class. Set out the supplies and be ready to welcome the children as they arrive.

Ask: Something is missing when you look at each of the pictures here. What is it? Can you finish the pictures?

Give the children time to finish each of the pictures. They will discover that in each of the pictures it is water that is missing.

Say: Water plays a very special part in today's Bible story. It takes on a very special meaning—one that is still with Christians today.

Supplies

Reproducible 4B, watercolor felt-tip markers, plastic dish pan, newspaper, an iron, paper towels, cotton swabs, plastic spoons or eye-droppers

Art Effects

Make a copy of the dove glider **(Reproducible 4B)** for each child in the group. This glider will be used in a game in the lesson, so it is important to do the decorating early to give the gliders time to dry. If you find the gliders are not dry by the time you are ready to fold them and fly them, place each piece of paper between paper towels and iron until it is dry. This will require adult supervision.

Have the children color their dove gliders using watercolor markers. Encourage each to cover the entire design. Then provide them an option as to how to use the water.

They may dip their entire papers into the dishpan of water and allow the colors to run together.

They may take cotton swabs and dip them into water, and then rub them over their designs.

A third choice might be to hold the paper with two hands, have a friend drip water onto it, and then tilt it back and forth to let the water run in pleasing ways.

Say: Not only do we hear a story from the Bible that talks about water being something very special, but we also learn how the dove became the symbol of our church for the Holy Spirit. All those who were present at Jesus' baptism in today's story knew that Jesus was God's Son.

> **Jesus is God's Son, the promised Savior.**

Are You the One?

Bring the children together in the storytelling area. Have the children sit in a circle either on the floor or in chairs. Have them put their hands in front of them in their laps, fingertips to fingertips, forming empty pockets between their hands. Select one child to be "IT" and come to the center of the group. Hold a small object (an eraser, paper clip, or small plastic block) in your two hands. Pass your hands through the hands of each child. Let the object drop into the hands of one of the children. Continue around the circle. Caution the children that the one with the object should not indicate that she or he has the object.

Say: The land of the Bible-times Hebrews was occupied by the Romans at the time when Jesus was born. Rome made the people pay heavy taxes. Rome set up regional governors who told the people what to do. Most of the time the people were miserable under Roman rule, because Romans did not believe in the one true God. The people remembered a time when their country was ruled by David and there was a time of prosperity. And they remembered God's promise to send them a Messiah, a Savior from the house of David who would rule them and bring about a time of peace and prosperity. They were always asking anyone who might be preaching the coming of God's kingdom: "Are you the one?"

Ask: Who was the Messiah? Who could it be? Was it John? Who was the one?

Let IT try to guess who has the object in his or her hands. IT can tap three people on the head, one at a time. Those people must open their hands to indicate what's inside. The person holding the object will become the next IT if IT discovers the object in her or his hands, and IT will take that person's place in the circle.

Say: The people watched carefully for any sign that the new king was born. The wise men saw the star, and they knew Jesus' birth had occurred. The people, however, still wondered who the Messiah could be after so many years of awaiting God's promise to be fulfilled.

Jesus is God's Son, the promised Savior.

John the Baptist Rap

by LeeDell Stickler

The story for today is done in a modified rap style. The rap does not rhyme except for the response the children will repeat. It does, however, have a distinctive rhythm. The pattern is done in two-line couplets:

Line 1: da da **DA** da da **DA** da da **DA** da
Line 2: da da **DA** da da **DA** da da **DA**

Let the children practice saying their part *(the four-line couplet written in boldface type)* in the rhythm.

In the Bible we read of a servant,
And the name he was given was John.
He lived far away in the desert,
There he preached a new message of love.
For this man was a voice crying out now,
A loud voice crying out to the world.
"Listen, sinners, the time's running out soon.
Let's repent before God's kingdom comes."

John the Baptist he stands by the river
Telling people they've got to repent.
John the Baptist he stands by the river,
Waiting for the Messiah God sent.

Now the people they came to the desert,
For they wanted to hear what John said.
"Tell us, John, could you be the Messiah?
Are you really the one that God sent?
If you're not then perhaps you're Elijah,
Or the prophet we're told to await."
But then John would just shake his head slowly,
Answer "No, I am only the voice."

John the Baptist he stands by the river
Telling people they've got to repent.
John the Baptist he stands by the river,
Waiting for the Messiah God sent.

44

"Listen up, and I'll give you the skinny,
I'm the voice but I'm not the true One.
What I say to the folks who will hear me,
'Repent and make straight the Lord's way.'
With the water the people I'll baptize.
But the one who is coming will not.
For I hear he will baptize with Spirit.
And will gather the children of God.

**John the Baptist he stands by the river
Telling people they've got to repent.
John the Baptist he stands by the river,
Waiting for the Messiah God sent.**

"He is coming some day, this I promise,
You don't know him right now, but you will.
I am sure that he lives here among us,
And we'll know when he thinks the time's right."
Then one day in the crowd at the river,
Preacher John saw a familiar face.
"There he is, he's the one that I told you.
Lamb of God, the Beloved, God's Son."

**John the Baptist he stands by the river
Telling people they've got to repent.
John the Baptist he stands by the river,
Waiting for the Messiah God sent.**

Jesus walked to the river with purpose,
Preacher John did just what Jesus asked.
And when he came up from the water,
What they heard filled the people with awe.
The heavens split open above him,
And God's Spirit came down like a dove.
A loud voice was then heard all about him.
"That's my Son, and with him I am pleased."

**John the Baptist he stands by the river
Telling people they've got to repent.
John the Baptist he stands by the river,
Waiting for the Messiah God sent.**

Stories of Jesus - Elementary

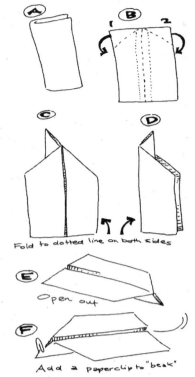

Glide On!

Supplies

Reproducible 4B, scissors, paper clip, masking tape

If you did the "Art Effects" activity, by this time the dove gliders should be dry. Show the children how to fold the gliders as indicated here.

Say: The dove has become the symbol of the Holy Spirit because of what happened to Jesus when he was baptized by John. *(Recall how the Holy Spirit came down on Jesus like a dove when he came up from the water after being baptized.)* **Let's play a game. Let's see if you can get your dove gliders to land in the circle that I will create on the floor from masking tape.**

Use masking tape to create a space on the floor. Make it large enough for the doves to fit inside. Pace off a distance of about six to ten feet. Mark a starting line at that point. The children can throw as often as they like, but they must stay behind the line. Whenever a child's dove lands inside the circle, the child will say: "Jesus is the Son of God."

If you have a large group you may want to create several circles and divide the children into groups of six participants. That way each child will have time to throw several times.

Remind the children that at Jesus' baptism God claimed Jesus as his Son. At this point the Bible tells us all about what Jesus said and did.

Sing and Celebrate

Supplies

None

Sing together the song "There Was a Man Named John" to the tune of "The Farmer in the Dell."

There Was a Man Named John
(Tune: "The Farmer in the Dell")

There was a man named John,
There was a man named John,
He preached down by the riverside.
There was a man named John.

Oh, Jesus came to John,
Oh, Jesus came to John,

He went down by the riverside.
Oh, Jesus came to John,

"This is the Son of God."
"This is the Son of God."
John said down by the riverside.
"This is the Son of God."

Spread the Word

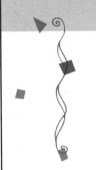

Ask: **What do you think happened when John told the people, "Here he is! This is the one! He's the one you've been waiting for!"** *(Invite the children to share what they think happened.)* **Do you think the word spread?**

Say: **Let's pretend that this dove glider is flying to tell the good news about Jesus. Let's see how long it will take us to get it all the way around the circle.** *(Start the glider with the child on your right. When it gets to the last person, have them stand up and say, "He's the One!")*

If you have a watch with a second hand, time the children to see how long it takes. Then do it again and see if the children can beat their own times.

If you do not have a watch, count in a slow, steady beat. Repeat the same beat when the children try again.

Say: **Certainly anyone who was there at the river who heard the voice from heaven declaring that Jesus was God's Son would have been pretty excited and eager to spread the word. Now Jesus had declared his mission had begun. From here on in he was on task for God.**

Dove Prayers

Hold up one of the dove gliders.

Say: **As we pass this dove glider around the circle today let's think about how exciting it must have been to be at that riverside when God claimed Jesus as God's Son.**

When the dove glider has made it all the way around the circle, have the children join hands and form a prayer circle.

Pray: **Dear God, we thank you for your Son, Jesus. We are glad you sent him to teach us more about you. Help us to listen and to be followers. Amen.**

> **Jesus is God's Son, the promised Savior.**

What's missing in each picture?
Finish each picture.

REPRODUCIBLE 4A

Permission granted to photocopy for local church use. © 1999, 2009 Abingdon Press.

ALL-IN-ONE BIBLE FUN

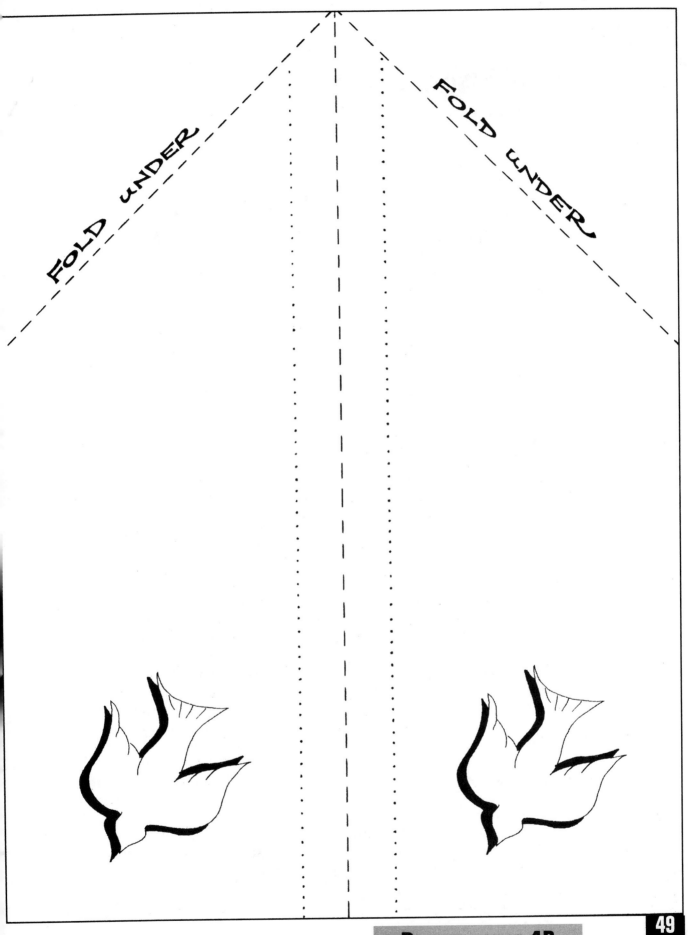

FOLD UNDER

FOLD UNDER

All-in-One
BIBLE ELEMENTARY
FUN

In the Desert

Bible Verse

Worship the Lord your God,
and serve only him.

Luke 4:8

Bible Story

Matthew 4:1-11; Mark 1:12-13; Luke 4:1-13

After Jesus was baptized, the Holy Spirit led him into the wilderness of Judea. There Jesus began a struggle: to serve God or to serve the world. A call to ministry or vocation often causes a struggle between the call and worldly considerations. The beginning of Jesus' ministry was marked by a particularly dramatic struggle.

The account of Jesus' encounter with Satan in the wilderness can be viewed as Jesus' struggle to establish a direction for his ministry. Certainly Jesus could easily have provided for his own physical needs. How much easier it would have been to attract followers if he had done something so dramatic as to throw himself down from the Temple and land without a single scratch! Seeking the political power of a mighty ruler would certainly be a heady experience. But Jesus had to keep in mind: God's kingdom was not a kingdom of the world. People had to accept his salvation through faith, not

through miraculous proof. And the physical needs of the world are small when placed in comparison to the riches of the Kingdom.

Throughout the temptations Jesus held firm. He never sought to glorify himself but chose to be God's servant. His ministry was more than one of miraculous events and spectacular deeds. Jesus always remained faithful to the will of God.

God gave each of us the power to choose. We can choose for good or we can choose for evil. Elementary children still live in a world that is centered around themselves. Every action or event is evaluated by children as it impacts him or her. This is as it should be, since children must rely on others for survival. But as they grow older, they will develop a sense of other. Sin occurs when persons put their own desires and their own needs above all else. As followers of Jesus we are called to be servants of God.

Jesus chose to serve and worship God; we can too.

If time is limited, we recommend those activities that are noted in **boldface**. Depending on your time and the number of children, you may be able to include more activities.

ACTIVITY	TIME	SUPPLIES	
What's Wrong Here?	**5 minutes**	**Reproducible 5A, pencils or crayons**	**JOIN THE FUN**
It's A-MAZE-ing	10 minutes	Reproducible 5B, plastic or paper drinking straws, white glue, scissors, strong cardboard sheets (approximately 8 inches by 12 inches) or small box lids	
King of the World	5 minutes	chairs	**BIBLE STORY FUN**
Bible Story: Good Guys vs. Bad Guys	**10 minutes**	**None**	
A-MAZE-ing Adventure	10 minutes	gameboard (Reproducible 5B), aluminum foil	
Sing and Celebrate	5 minutes	None	
Lamb and Wolf	5 minutes	None	**LIVE THE FUN**
Bible Prayers	**5 minutes**	**Bible**	

JOIN THE FUN

Supplies

Reproducible 5A, pencils or crayons

What's Wrong Here?

Make a copy of the mixed-up picture **(Reproducible 5A)** for each child in the class. Greet the children as they arrive. Make them feel welcome.

Ask: Would you rather do something right or something wrong? Why or why not?

Say: Most people want to do what's right. But let's face it—sometimes, we are very tempted to do what's wrong. Would you believe that even Jesus, God's own Son, was tempted to do wrong? But he made the right decision: to love and serve God. Let's see how many "wrong" things you can find in this picture.

> **Jesus chose to serve and worship God; we can too.**

Supplies

Reproducible 5B, plastic or paper drinking straws, white glue, scissors, strong cardboard sheets (approximately 8 inches by 12 inches) or small box lids

It's A-MAZE-ing

Give each child a copy of the gameboard **(Reproducible 5B)**, a sheet of strong cardboard or small box lid, and about twenty drinking straws.

Say: As we go through life we are going to come across things that will tempt us to do wrong. It is our individual responsibility to avoid these traps. We are going to create a game that will remind us to love and serve God and avoid the temptation to do wrong.

Mount the gameboard on a piece of cardboard or in a box lid. Cut drinking straws the length of the lines. Run a thin line of glue down the lines, then place the straw on the lines. When all the lines are covered set aside the gameboard to allow it to dry.

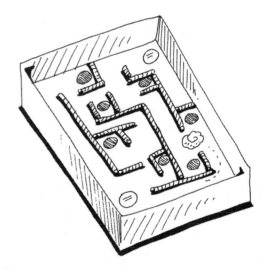

52

King of the World

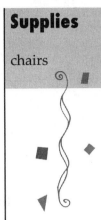

Bring the children together in the storytelling or worship area.

Ask: What would you do if you were "King of the World"? *(Invite the children to share their dreams.)*

Say: Jesus was given an opportunity to be just that, but he turned it down. He turned it down because he knew that was not why God had sent him into the world. Here was Jesus with all the power of God at his command—and yet he never once used his power to do things that would make himself look good. He only did things that would glorify God.

Ask: How strong do you have to be in order to be powerful? *(Invite the children to share their ideas.)* **Do you have to be as strong as a muscle man? a football player? a wrestler? Superman?**

Say: You can be powerful using just your little pinky finger.

Divide the children into pairs. Have one person sit in a chair with his or her back up against the back of the chair. Have the person who is standing gently put their pinky finger on the person's forehead. Tell the persons in the chair to stand up. They will not be able to stand up without moving forward, and the pinky finger will keep them from moving forward. Then have the children swap places and try again.

Say: Jesus was very powerful and yet he didn't use his power except to help people. You don't have to be very strong to be powerful. We are powerful too because we love God and serve God.

Jesus chose to serve and worship God; we can too.

Good Guys vs. Bad Guys

by LeeDell Stickler

Say: All of us are tempted to do wrong once in a while. We can all hear that little Bad Guy voice inside of us that says, "Go on. Do it!" And then we can hear that other little Good Guy voice that says, "Don't do it!" I would imagine that maybe Jesus also heard those voices inside when he was tempted to do what was wrong. As I tell today's story you are going to act as those voices. When we lean to the right, that's the Good Guy voice. Every one will say: "Remember, you're God's Son. Don't do it!" Then when we lean to the left, that's the Bad Guy voice. Everyone will say: "Remember, you're God's Son. Do it!"

Let the children practice linking elbows around the circle, leaning first to the right, then to the left, and have them say the appropriate expression. Signal the children by pausing at the appropriate time in the story.

Select one person to read the part of Satan and one person to read the part of Jesus. Make sure the readers are confident readers—or you can invite a youth to play the two roles.

Reader #1: The time had come for Jesus to claim his birthright. The word was out. All those who had gathered at the river that day had heard the voice of God. God claimed Jesus as his very own Son. Now, what to do next? Jesus took himself out into the wilderness to be alone for awhile and think. For forty days Jesus had eaten nothing; he had drunk nothing. So there he was, at his very weakest, hungry and thirsty, and that was when it happened. Jesus heard the voice of temptation.

Satan: Hey, man! I'll bet you're hungry. No problem. You're the Son of God. Take those rocks there and turn them into crispy, brown bread. You can do it, you know.

Reader #2: But Jesus knew that if he gave in to this temptation he would be using God's power for his *own* needs. And that is *not* why God sent him. So Jesus answered him …

Jesus: A person does not live by bread alone but by the very word of God.

ALL-IN-ONE BIBLE FUN

Satan: Oh come on, man. Look around you. If you really are who you say you are, prove it. Throw yourself off this high place. I know God will protect you. Not a hair on your head will be harmed. Do it!

Lean to the right; lean to the left.

Reader #3: But Jesus knew that if he gave in to this he would be using his power to show off. He would be glorifying *himself* and not *God*. So Jesus answered him …

Jesus: I don't have to prove myself to you or to anyone.

Satan: OK, but I want you to look around you. See all the world. See all the people down there. See all those great cities. If you will just bow down to me and worship me, just a little bit, just one time, then I will give you all of this. You won't have to work at it—this will be all yours.

Lean to the right; lean to the left.

Reader #4: But Jesus knew that there was only one God. To bow down and worship anyone or any-thing else would be the greatest sin. And so Jesus answered him …

Jesus: Get away from me, you evil person. I will worship God and only God.

Reader #5: And knowing that the battle to win Jesus over to the side of the evil one was lost, Satan left. Then God sent angels to care for Jesus.

Ask: What were the three things Satan wanted Jesus to do? *(turn rocks into bread, throw himself off the ledge, worship Satan)* **Did Jesus do any of those things?** *(no)* **Why not?** *(Because Jesus knew that God had sent him on a special mission and his purpose was to serve and glorify only God.)* **Have you ever been tempted to do something you know is wrong? Did you resist it? Did you know that God will help you resist temptation if you ask for God's help?**

Supplies

gameboard (Reproducible 5B), aluminum foil

A-MAZE-ing Adventure

Give each child his or her A-MAZE-ing gameboard **(Reproducible 5B)**. Cut aluminum foil into six-inch squares. Have the children wad up the aluminum foil until it forms a small ball. The more tightly packed the ball, the easier it will be to move it through the maze.

Say: We are tempted to do things we know we shouldn't do every day of our lives—no matter how old or young we may be. *(Identify the various activities on the gameboard that are temptations children at this age may face—saying naughty words, stealing, hitting, defacing other's property, telling a lie, gossiping, not attending church).* **In this maze you are to try to move your aluminum foil ball from the start to the finish and not let it fall into any of the temptations. Every time your ball finds itself in one of those traps you will get a point. The object is to get through with as few points as possible. Do it one time, then do it again to see if you can make a better score.**

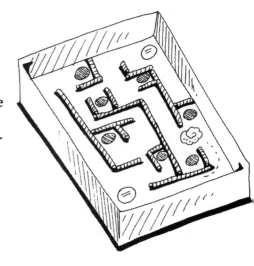

Point out to the children that this game should remind them that everyone is tempted to do wrong. Even Jesus was tempted, but the real success is to resist temptation.

Supplies

None

Sing and Celebrate

Sing together the song "Worship the Lord" to the tune of "God Is So Good." Help the children identify the words from today's Bible verse, "Worship the Lord your God, / and serve only him" (Luke 4:8).

Worship the Lord
(Tune: "God Is So Good")

Worship the Lord.
Worship the Lord.
Worship the Lord.
And serve only him.

Jesus chose to serve and worship God; we can too.

Lamb and Wolf

Supplies

None

Say: We know that we are tempted to do wrong. But God will help us resist temptation. God cares about us and will strengthen us during times when we are tempted to do wrong. Let's play a game where a big, bad wolf will represent the terrible things we may be tempted to do. The wolf is trying to get at the sweet lamb. But those of us in the circle are going to try to protect the lamb and help the lamb just as God protects and helps us.

Have the children come to the open area of the room and form a circle, holding hands. Select one person to be the lamb. The lamb will stand inside the circle. Select a second person to be the wolf. The wolf must remain outside the circle. The object of the game is for the wolf to try to capture the lamb by touching the lamb on the shoulder. The lamb will be assisted by those in the circle, who will attempt to keep the wolf out and allow the lamb to come and go at will. Persons in the circle may raise and lower their arms in an attempt to hinder the wolf and help the lamb. To make the game more exciting you may have two wolves and two lambs. When the lamb is caught, he or she may become the wolf and select another child to be the lamb. Or, two new children may be selected to continue the game.

Play until everyone has had a chance to be either the lamb or the wolf or until the children get bored.

Bible Prayers

Supplies

Bible

Show the children the Bible.

Say: Jesus used words from Scripture to help him resist temptation. Today we want to think about all the times we are tempted to do wrong. As I pass this Bible around the circle, think to yourself of something you really need help resisting. Then when we have a quiet time during the prayer, ask God to help you with this. *(Pass the Bible around the circle. When it has been all the way around have the children bow their heads.)*

Pray: Dear God, we know that you can help us whenever we are tempted to do wrong, just as you helped Jesus be strong. Help us be strong whenever we are tempted to do wrong. *(Pause and let each child share his or her own weaknesses with God.)* **Amen.**

> Jesus chose to serve and worship God; we can too.

57

What's Wrong With This Picture?

REPRODUCIBLE 5A

ALL-IN-ONE BIBLE FUN

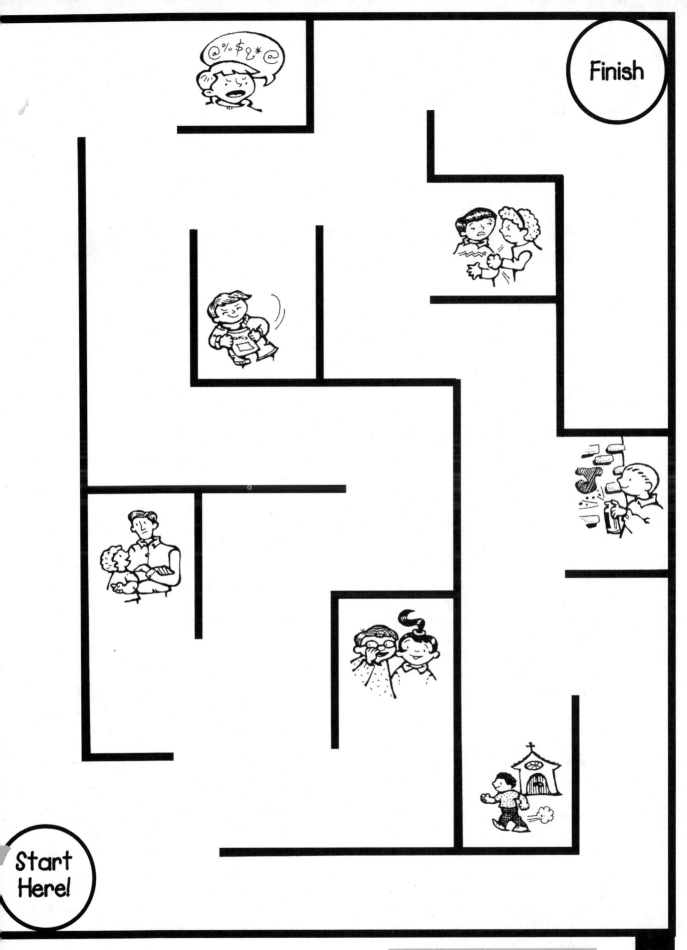

All-in-One
BIBLE ELEMENTARY
FUN

At the Synagogue

Bible Verse

The Spirit of the Lord is upon me.

Luke 4:18

Bible Story

Matthew 13:54-58; Mark 6:1-6; Luke 4:16-30

We all know the old saying, "familiarity breeds contempt." This certainly applies to the opening stages of Jesus' ministry in his hometown of Nazareth. Jesus' friends and neighbors may have thought something like this: "Here is the carpenter's son, a quite likeable fellow. He comes from good stock, but now he's becoming a little pretentious. What makes him think he understands God better than we do?"

The rejection of Jesus' ministry by those who had seen him grow up was not surprising. They thought they knew who Jesus was, but they had not recognized Jesus' special relationship with God. Jesus had been baptized by John, affirmed by God, and then he had struggled with Satan in the wilderness. He could not be the same after these events. The people of Nazareth could not understand the seeming change in the Jesus they thought they knew, and they misinterpreted the change.

Jesus announced the beginning of his ministry in the synagogue at Nazareth. His message would be to the poor and the oppressed. This was a message people were not eager to hear—and they certainly did not want to hear it from this man who was one of their own.

Jesus' rejection by the people in his hometown is something we all struggle with. If we are called to minister in ways that make our friends and relatives uncomfortable, we too may face the same type of rejection. It takes great strength and firm belief in the will of God to face being rejected by loved ones.

Look around you at the children in your class. Which of them might grow up to be a doctor or a teacher or a physicist? Are there some who might be preachers, or who might bring the word of God to persons far across the globe? Thank God for the world leaders you may already know.

God sent Jesus to bring good news to all people.

If time is limited, we recommend those activities that are noted in **boldface**. Depending on your time and the number of children, you may be able to include more activities.

ACTIVITY	TIME	SUPPLIES
Good News Rally	**5 minutes**	**Reproducible 6A, pencils or crayons**
Shoebox Shuffle	10 minutes	two shoeboxes for each team, envelopes, index cards, felt-tip markers
Truth or Lie?	10 minutes	None
Bible Story: Riots in Nazareth!	**10 minutes**	**None**
Good News Race	15 minutes	Reproducible 6B, crayons or felt-tip markers, scissors, two chairs per team, string, white glue or tape, masking tape
Sing and Celebrate	5 minutes	None
Hand Talk Prayer	**5 minutes**	**Bible**

Good News Rally

Make a copy of the Good News Rally **(Reproducible 6A)** for each child in the class. Greet the children as they arrive. Try to say something personal to each child.

Say: The boys and girls in this puzzle want everyone to know the good news about Jesus. Can you get the good news to each person pictured here? In today's Bible story we learn that God sent Jesus to bring good news to the people.

> **God sent Jesus to bring good news to all people.**

Shoebox Shuffle

Divide the children into teams of four or more children. Each team will need an assembler for the Bible verse. You will need to make a set of envelopes for each team of children. Each set of envelopes consists of five index cards and five envelopes. On each index card write one word or group of words from the Bible verse as shown here: "The Spirit," "of the Lord," "is," "upon," "me." Place a card inside each envelope and seal it. Color-code the envelopes for each team.

Say: The Bible tells us the good news about Jesus. We want other people to hear this good news as well. The object of this game is for each team to go to the post office, get an envelope that is designed for that team and bring it back to the assembler. When the team has assembled the entire Bible verse, then everyone will stand up and shout: "The Spirit of the Lord is upon me!"

Indicate one table to be the post office. Scatter all the color-coded envelopes on the table so that they are within reach.

Give each team two shoe boxes. The runner for each team must put the shoe boxes on his or her feet, shuffle to the post office, pick up one of the team's letters (indicated by color), and shuffle back to the team. Then the next person on the team will put on the shoe boxes and repeat the process. The first team to get the Bible verse assembled will win the game.

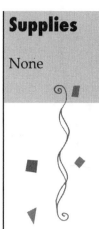

Truth or Lie?

Bring the children together in the storytelling area. They may sit in chairs or on the floor.

Say: It wasn't easy to get the good news out today—and in Jesus' time this was even harder. One thing made it even more difficult. The people who were present when Jesus announced his relationship to God were people whom Jesus had known all of his life. They were his neighbors from when he was a boy. They were friends of his mother's and they were people who had come to Joseph to get things built. And then in the story Jesus said something that was totally inexcusable.

Ask: Have you ever had it happen to you that people who know you don't think you can possibly do anything special?

Say: Let's play a game. I want you to get into pairs. One of you will be Partner A. The other will be Partner B. Sit on the floor facing each other with your feet extended straight out in front of you. Partner A's feet will be up against Partner B's feet. Partner A will tell something about himself or herself. It can be true or it can be made up. If Partner B thinks it is true, Partner B will say, "I believe it." If Partner B thinks the statement is false, Partner B will say, "Liar, liar, pants on fire." If Partner B says "Liar, liar, pants on fire" and the statement is true, it will be Partner A's turn to listen.

Play for several minutes, encouraging the children to come up with some things about themselves that no one would know. When it looks like everyone has had a chance, bring the children back to the circle.

Ask: What did you learn? *(that there are many things about each other with which they are unfamiliar)* **Do you think that same sort of thing happened to Jesus? Did people learn something about him that they hadn't known before?**

Say: Now listen in today's Bible story and find out what thing Jesus said that made everyone angry.

God sent Jesus to bring good news to all people.

Riots in Nazareth!

by LeeDell Stickler

Today's Bible story is done in the format of a fast-breaking news story on CNN. Select children who are confident readers to play the various parts, or invite older children from another class to be the characters. You will need these persons: BNN (Bible News Network) Reporter, Elder of the synagogue, Neighbor, Synagogue Member, Crowd Members #1 and #2. Make a copy of the script. Highlight each child's part.

Ask: Have you ever wondered what the people who grew up around Jesus must have thought about him? What about his neighbors? What about the other townsfolk of Nazareth?

Say: I think you might be surprised. Let's listen in on a fast-breaking news story that is coming out of Nazareth.

BNN Reporter: This is BNN in Nazareth. We've heard rumors of a riot, but nothing has been confirmed. I see a man standing nearby. He appears to be in shock. Excuse me, sir, could you shed some light on the riot story?

Synagogue Member: It was terrible, just terrible. And to think it happened on the sabbath day.

BNN Reporter: Can you tell us how it all got started?

Synagogue Member: We had gathered at the synagogue as is our custom. Everyone in the village was there. The word got around that Jesus, one of our hometown boys, was going to be there. We've been hearing a great deal about him lately.

BNN Reporter: Did he start the riot?

Neighbor: He might as well have!

BNN Reporter: Would you like to tell us more about that?

Neighbor: Well, I mean, really! It's not as if we didn't know him. This was Jesus, Joseph the carpenter's son.

Elder: Now wait just a minute. You're skipping the best part.

BNN Reporter: Can you fill us in?

Elder: It started when I saw him come into the room.

BNN Reporter: Jesus?

Elder: That's the one! I recognized him so I asked if he would like to be the reader of the Scriptures at the worship. I gave him the scroll of Isaiah, the prophet.

BNN Reporter: Did he read it?

Neighbor: That was what started it all. He read it. He read the part about the promise of a Messiah. And when he sat down, he said that it was him. Give me a break.

Crowd Member #2: Yes, that's when everyone began to get a little testy.

BNN Reporter: Is that when the riot started?

Crowd Member #1: That was later. At first we were in shock! This was Jesus, Joseph's son. And he was claiming to be the Messiah.

Crowd Member #2: But you have to admit, we've heard stories about the things he has done in other cities.

Crowd Member #1: Well, did he do any of that here? No! Aren't we good enough?

BNN Reporter: But the riot! When did it start?

Elder: It started when Jesus told the crowd that God wasn't sending the Messiah to them exclusively, but to everyone. I think that was the last straw.

BNN Reporter: Is that when the riot started?

Crowd Member #2: That was when everyone rushed Jesus out to the edge of the city. They were so mad! I believe they were going to throw him over the edge of the cliff.

BNN Reporter: And is that when the riot happened?

Crowd Member #1: Well, all of a sudden Jesus was gone. He must have walked through the crowd when no one was watching.

BNN Reporter: No riot?

All: No!

BNN Reporter: No riot. No one thrown off a cliff. All right folks, let's pack up and get back to the station.

65

BIBLE STORY FUN

Supplies

Reproducible 6B, crayons or felt-tip markers, scissors, two chairs per team, string, white glue or tape, masking tape

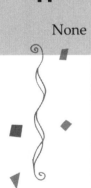

Good News Race

Divide the children into teams of two. Give each team a set of the Good News Race figures **(Reproducible 6B)**. Each team member will select one of the figures to represent herself or himself (Racey Rabbit or Turbo Turtle). Have the children decorate their figures as they choose.

Cut apart the two figures on the solid line. Fold on the dotted line. Cut out the two strips at the bottom of the page. Glue or tape the ends of each strip together forming a loop. Tape the loop to the inside of the rabbit or turtle card, making sure the loop extends above the card. Then tape or glue the sides together forming one figure with a loop at the top. This will provide the relay figure for the game.

Say: God sent Jesus to bring good news to the poor and the outcast. Jesus has given us the job of getting the good news to all persons all over the world. Let's have a race and see if Racey Rabbit and Turbo Turtle can get the good news moving.

Cut two pieces of yarn the same length (about ten feet). Place two chairs side by side. Attach yarn to the top rung of of each of the chairs. Thread the loop of the racing figure onto the yarn. Then attach the yarn to the second chair, taping it securely in place. Make sure both sets of chairs are side by side and the same distance apart. Make sure the string is fairly tight so that the figures can slide along the string easily. When the teacher shouts, "Go!" each team member will begin to blow on his or her figure. The first figure to reach the opposite chair wins the race.

Sing and Celebrate

Supplies

None

Sing together the song "Do You Know the Promised One?" to the tune of "Do You Know the Muffin Man?"

Do You Know the Promised One?
(Tune: "Do You Know the Muffin Man?")

Teacher:
Do you know the promised one,
The promised one, the promised one?
Do you know the promised one
That God sent to us all?

Children:
Yes, I know the promised one,
The promised one, the promised one.
Yes, I know the promised one
That God sent to us all.

All:
Jesus is the promised one,
The promised one, the promised one.
Jesus is the promised one
That God sent to us all.

Sing additional verses, letting the children make up the words to describe Jesus such as "the one God sent" or "the special king."

Words: Daphna Flegal

66

Hand Talk Prayer

Say: The prophet Isaiah in the scroll from which Jesus read said that the coming Messiah would have the Spirit of the Lord upon him and he would bring good news to the poor. We, too, have the Spirit of the Lord on us whenever we try to live as Jesus taught.

Teach the children signs from American Sign Language for the Bible verse for today. Let them practice until it comes easily.

Spirit—right palm above and facing the left palm with fingers spread; as the right hand moves up, the index and thumb tips of both hands close.
of—Hook right index finger and thumb into left index finger and thumb.
Lord—Place the right "L" at the left shoulder, then on the right waist.
is—Move pinky finger back and forth.
(up)on—palm of right open hand placed on back of the left open hand.
me—Point the right index finger at yourself.

Say: Think of something you can do this week to bring good news to others as I pass the Bible around today. Then we will all respond with the Bible verse for today.

Close with this prayer when everyone has had a chance to contribute.

Pray: Dear God, we thank you for Jesus, who brought good news to all people. Help us to follow his example. Amen.

God sent Jesus to bring good news to all people.

Good News Rally

Can you get the Good News of Jesus to everyone here?

REPRODUCIBLE 6A

Permission granted to photocopy for local church use. © 1999, 2009 Abingdon Press.

ALL-IN-ONE BIBLE FUN

All-in-One
BIBLE ELEMENTARY
FUN

By the Sea

Bible Verse

Come with me, and I will teach you to catch people.

Matthew 4:19, GNT

Bible Story

Matthew 4:18-22; Mark 1:16-20; Luke 5:1-11

Jesus went to the city of Capernaum after his rejection at Nazareth. He recruited his first disciples from the shores of the Sea of Galilee. Disciples of great teachers were not uncommon in Bible times. Boys would often associate themselves with a teacher whose life was dedicated to teaching and meditation, after years of study. These boys would become "disciples" of the teacher. Teachers commonly called talented students to be their disciples. It was, however, uncommon for a teacher to call those who did not seem to have great affinity for lifelong study. Certainly the persons Jesus called fell into the latter category.

Jesus called workingmen and -women to be his followers. We often talk about the "poor" fishermen. But these were busy men who made a living from fishing. They were working-class people. They may not have been not rich, but they had full lives. The extraordinary thing is that these ordinary men left jobs, families, and possessions to learn at the feet of Jesus and to pass on that learning after his death. Earning a living and building ordinary lives would no longer be the focus of the new disciples' lives. The disciples would travel with Jesus after their call; from now on they would depend upon the hospitality of others.

The four fishermen that Jesus called from the Sea of Galilee (Peter, Andrew, James, and John) became his core group. By the time of Jesus' death he had many "disciples," or persons who followed him wherever he went. In order to set this group apart the first twelve disciples are often referred to as the twelve apostles. We often tell children that they too can become disciples of Jesus. They may wonder how this can happen. The answer lies in belief in Jesus as the Son of God and the attempt to follow Jesus' teachings. Even the youngest of children can be "disciples" of Jesus.

Jesus called disciples to help him spread the Good News.

If time is limited, we recommend those activities that are noted in **boldface**. Depending on your time and the number of children, you may be able to include more activities.

ACTIVITY	TIME	SUPPLIES	
How Many Fish?	**5 minutes**	**Reproducible 7A, crayons or felt-tip markers**	JOIN THE FUN
Swim Fish, Swim	10 minutes	masking tape	
Disciples Grab	10 minutes	brown paper bag, masking tape, crayons or small plastic blocks in different colors	BIBLE STORY FUN
Bible Story: "Follow Me!"	**10 minutes**	**Reproducible 7B, strips of paper or index cards, tape or glue, scissors**	
Let's Go Fishin'	15 minutes	Reproducible 7B, paper clips, crayons or felt-tip markers, tape or glue, newspaper, yarn or string, scissors, blue fabric or paper, pennies or metal washers	
Sing and Celebrate	5 minutes	None	
Join the Disciple-Ship	5 minutes	masking tape	LIVE THE FUN
Fish Prayers	**5 minutes**	**fish (Reproducible 7B)**	

JOIN THE FUN

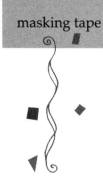

Supplies

Reproducible 7A, crayons or felt-tip markers

How Many Fish?

Make a copy of the hidden fish puzzle (**Reproducible 7A**) for each child in the room. Greet the children as they arrive.

Say: We learn as we talk about Jesus that he needed people to help him spread the good news. But Jesus chose ordinary workingmen to be his first disciples instead of choosing scholarly students like many teachers of the time period.

Ask: I wonder what people would do today if Jesus asked them to drop everything and follow him? Would we drop everything, leave our homes and our families and travel about learning from Jesus? What do you think?

> **Jesus called disciples to help him spread the Good News.**

Supplies

masking tape

Swim Fish, Swim

Say: The first persons Jesus chose to be his helpers were four fishermen who had small fishing businesses on the Sea of Galilee. Fish was a major food for people in Bible times. The job of a fisherman was very important because of this. There were no refrigerators or freezers, so fresh fish had to be caught every day. These fishermen used large nets to catch their fish rather than using fishing poles and bait. Sometimes they threw the nets out from the shore. Other times they threw the nets out from their boats on the lake.

Create safe harbors on opposite sides of the room using masking tape. Have all the children line up horizontally at one side of the playing area behind the masking tape line. Choose one player to be the fisherman. The fisherman will stand in the center of the playing area and call out: "I'm a fisherman as you can see. So come, little fish, come swimming to me." All the players will then run to the opposite side of the area. Those tagged by the fisherman join hands and then form a "net" to catch the other fish. Only the two ends may then tag, and the net must not be broken. Fish may swim through the net in the center and to the other side if not tagged. The last one caught is the fisherman for the next game.

72

Disciples Grab

brown paper bag, masking tape, crayons or small plastic blocks in different colors

Separate the crayons or small plastic blocks by color such as red, blue, yellow, and green before class. *(This would be a good arrival activity for children who get there extra early.)* If you have a small class, put only two colors of crayons or blocks in the bag. If you have a large class, put in four or more colors.

Make sure there is an even number of each color, or as much as possible according to the number of children who usually attend. Shake the bag and mix up all the crayons or blocks.

Bring the children together in the storytelling area.

Say: **When Jesus began his ministry he knew that he would need helpers. He only had a short time to get the Good News out to all people. It was common for a teacher in Bible times to call students to come and learn. What was uncommon was that the people Jesus called already had jobs and families and lifestyles. The disciples had to give up all these things and travel about with Jesus in order to follow him.**

Select two, four, or six "Teachers" from the group, depending on the size of the group you teach.

Say: **Each of these Teachers is looking for disciples. But they are looking for certain kinds of disciples. The Teachers will draw a crayon or block from the bag. Then, after everyone else has drawn from the bag, the Teachers will go in search of their disciples—all those who have the same color. If the Teacher finds you and says, "Follow me," then you will get in line behind him or her, holding onto his or her waist, and continue the search for disciples. That group will come to the storytelling area when each Teacher thinks he or she has found all the disciples that belong to him or her.**

Collect the crayons or blocks in the sack when all the disciples have been found.

Jesus called disciples to help him spread the Good News.

"Follow Me!"

by LeeDell Stickler

Make a copy of the disciple names (**Reproducible 7B**). Cut them out and tape or glue them on strips of paper or index cards. Hand out the names to twelve children. Let some children hold more than one disciple's name if you have fewer than twelve in class.

Say: Whenever we come to the phrase, "Follow me!" each of you in turn will hold up your paper and say the name, until all twelve disciples are named.

Jesus left his hometown of Nazareth and went to live in the town of Capernaum, a town on the shore of Lake Galilee. From there Jesus began to preach his message: Turn away from your sins because the kingdom of God is near.

Soon Jesus began to realize that he needed helpers if he were to do all that God required of him. But who could Jesus invite? Who could he ask to come and learn from him so that they could carry on the message after he was gone? Who would he ask to **"Follow me!"**?

One day as Jesus saw two brothers who were fishermen as he walked along the shore of Lake Galilee. One of the brothers was called Simon. (He was also called Peter.) Standing with Peter in the boat was his brother Andrew. They had just come in from fishing all night and were rolling up their nets.

Jesus came up to them. "If you will come with me, I will teach you to catch people instead of fish."

Andrew rolled up his net and put it in the boat. Peter hung the fishing gear on the side of the boat, and both men left their nets and went with Jesus.

Peter and Andrew, these were the first to answer when Jesus said **"Follow me!"**

ALL-IN-ONE BIBLE FUN

Jesus and Peter and Andrew continued walking down the lakeside. They came upon two other brothers. James and John were the sons of Zebedee. The two were helping their father repair their nets from the night's fishing.

Jesus called out to them, "Put down your nets and come with me. I will teach you to catch people instead."

At once James and John put down their nets, waved at their father, and went with Jesus.

James and John were two more people who answered when Jesus said, **"Follow me!"**

Now Jesus had four disciples. But this was not enough. Time was short and there was much to do.

On and on Jesus went. Whenever he came to a person he thought would be a good disciple, Jesus said to that individual, **"Follow me!"** And the person did.

Soon Jesus had twelve disciples all together. Wherever Jesus went, his disciples went with him. They ate together, and they talked together. But most important, Jesus taught them all they would need to know so that later, after he had gone, they could teach others about him. They would say to those people just as Jesus had said to them, **"Follow me!"**

Supplies

Reproducible 7B, paper clips, crayons or felt-tip markers, tape or glue, newspaper, yarn or string, scissors, blue fabric or paper, pennies or metal washers

Let's Go Fishin'

Make three copies of the Disciple Fish **(Reproducible 7B)** for each team of children. If you have a small class make a complete set for each child. Divide the children into teams of four children. If you have a very small group each child can fish for himself or herself. Have the children cut out the Disciple Fish squares and the disciple names. Children will color the fish and then attach two of the same disciple names *(one on the right side; one on the left side)* to their Disciple Fish. Fold the fish along the dotted lines. This will make a flat bottom. Tape one or two pennies or metal washers to the bottom of each fish so that it will stand up. Tape or glue together the top edges of the Disciple Fish together. You will now have a triangle-shaped piece that sits on a flat bottom. Attach a partially opened paper clip to the top of the piece.

To make a fishing pole: Tightly roll a single sheet of newspaper. Then tape at the top, the bottom, and in the middle so that the pole doesn't come undone. Tie a twenty-four inch piece of string to the end of the pole. To the end of the string, tie another partially opened paper clip.

The object of the game is for each team (or child) to "catch" the twelve disciples. As each Disciple Fish is caught, the team member brings it back to the group, the name is crossed off the list, and another team member "goes fishing." When all twelve disciples have been caught for each team, the fishing tournament is over.

Supplies

None

Sing and Celebrate

Sing together the song "Four Fishermen" to the tune of "London Bridge."

Four Fishermen
(Tune: "London Bridge")

Jesus called four fishermen,
Fishermen, fishermen.
Jesus called four fishermen
To fish for people now.

I can fish for people too,
People too, people too.
I can fish for people too
And tell you God loves you.

Words: Daphna Flegal © 1998 Abingdon Press.

Join the Disciple-Ship

Make the shape of a ship on the floor out of masking tape. Make sure it is big enough for everyone in the class to stand inside.

Say: Jesus called disciples in Bible times to help him spread the Good News. Jesus calls disciples today, too. Jesus wants us to spread the Good News. Here on the floor I've made an outline of a ship, a Disciple-Ship. We are living as disciples of Jesus whenever we try to live as Jesus taught, and whenever we follow Jesus' example. We are aboard the Disciple-Ship. I want you to think of some way you can be a disciple of Jesus in the coming week. As you think of something shout it out and I will invite you to "Get on board." We will all cheer when everyone is on the Disciple-Ship.

Let the children make suggestions. Give them some hints if they seem to have a difficult time: sharing toys, caring for persons who are sick, helping older persons, doing an act of kindness, saying something nice to another person, and so forth.

Fish Prayers

Supplies

fish (Reproducible 7B)

Have the children sit in a circle inside the Disciple-Ship. Hold up one of the fish from "Let's Go Fishin'" (**Reproducible 7B**).

Say: Today as we pass this fish around the circle I want you to think about what it must have been like to be called by Jesus. Jesus asked the disciples to leave everything that was familiar—their jobs and their families— and to come with him. He would teach them to catch people.

Have the children link hands when the fish has gone all the way around the circle.

Pray: Dear God, we are glad that Jesus asked disciples to help him spread the good news. We want to be disciples of Jesus, too. Show us the way. Amen.

> Jesus called disciples to help him spread the Good News.

How many fish can you find?

Jesus said, "Come with me, and I will teach you to catch people."
Matthew 4:19, GNT

REPRODUCIBLE 7A

ALL-IN-ONE BIBLE FUN

DISCIPLE FISH

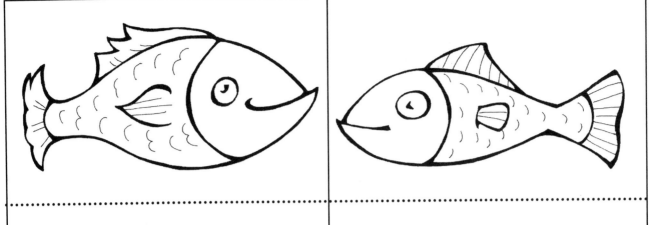

Peter	Andrew	James
Simon	Philip	John
James	Thaddeus	Matthew
Judas	Bartholomew	Thomas

79

Stories of Jesus - Elementary

All-in-One
BIBLE ELEMENTARY
FUN

On the Hillside

Bible Verse

Listen to what you are taught.
Be wise; do not neglect it.

Proverbs 8:33, GNT

Bible Story

Matthew 5:1-12; Luke 6:20-26

The Scripture references for today's lesson are a collection of Jesus' teachings that told people how to be truly happy. The longer version of similar teachings from the Book of Matthew is referred to as the Sermon on the Mount. These teachings follow Jesus' choosing of the inner circle of the disciples. Scholars continue to argue about whether the teachings from the Sermon on the Mount were given all at one time on a hillside, or whether they were collected and compiled from teachings at different times.

The first group of powerful sayings (called the Beatitudes) relates to the nature of happiness. Their overall meaning is that we must adjust our attitudes toward life and about God from our present attitudes to the ones God wants us to have. The teachings in question turned worldly thinking upside down. How can being poor be good? These sayings of Jesus forced persons to rethink their most basic reactions to events.

The second group of teachings deal with the nature of discipleship—love your enemy; do not judge others; lend without expecting anything in return; forgive and you will be forgiven; do to others as you would have them do to you. Jesus' words shocked the people of his day, just as surely as persons today regard these teachings with a degree of skepticism. But Jesus wanted to be very clear: All who want to be true disciples must live by these teachings. We are not true disciples if we are called into a relationship with Jesus, but refuse to live out Jesus' teachings in our relationships with others.

Children need to see us modeling these qualities of discipleship. They need to see adults who are striving to live as Jesus lived. They need to see how parents and other significant role models can love their enemies and care for the needs of others. And we need to affirm such behavior in our own children when we see it.

Jesus teaches us how to live.

If time is limited, we recommend those activities that are noted in **boldface**. Depending on your time and the number of children, you may be able to include more activities.

ACTIVITY	TIME	SUPPLIES	
A Tree and Its Fruit	**10 minutes**	**Reproducible 8A, Bible, crayons or felt-tip markers**	JOIN THE FUN
Get the Message	10 minutes	ball for each team	
Words to the Wise	10 minutes	Reproducible 8B, lunch-size paper bags, newspaper, construction paper (brown, yellow, black), rubber bands, white glue or tape	BIBLE STORY FUN
Bible Story: Sermon on the Mount	**5 minutes**	**Reproducible 8B, scissors**	
Fruitful Actions	10 minutes	Reproducible 8C, scissors, masking tape	
Sing and Celebrate	5 minutes	None	
Scripture Scramble	5 minutes	Words to the Wise (Reproducible 8B); sheet, blanket, or blindfold	LIVE THE FUN
Growing Up Prayers	**5 minutes**	**Bible**	

A Tree and Its Fruit

Make a copy of the Bible verse puzzle **(Reproducible 8A)**. You may want to mark the Bible verses ahead of time if you have a group of mostly younger elementary children, or pair younger children with older children to do the activity.

Each verse on the basket is missing a word. The children are to look up the verse, discover the missing word, and color the apple as indicated on the basket.

Say: God sent Jesus into the world to teach the people the things God called them to be and to do. Throughout the Bible we find verses that give people this message. These verses on the puzzle are just some of the messages that God wanted the people to know.

> **Jesus teaches us how to live.**

Get the Message

Divide the children into two teams. Have the players sit side by side on the floor with legs extended, facing the opposite team. The first player in each line will be given a ball.

At a signal, the player will put the ball on his or her feet (feet will be close together). Then, using only the player's feet, that player will transfer the ball to the tops of the feet of the next player in line. The ball will be passed in this manner all the way to the end of the line and back again.

If the ball drops the last player to have possession of the ball will have to pick it up with his or her own feet before continuing. The winning team will be the first one to successfully get the ball all the way up and down the line.

When the game is over ask the children: **Was it easy to get the ball up and down the line?** *(No)*

Say: Think of the ball as the message that Jesus was trying to get to the people. It wasn't easy to get the message to the people. The message was different from what they were used to hearing, and sometimes the people wondered how all the parts of Jesus' teachings could fit together.

Words to the Wise

Supplies

Reproducible 8B, lunch-size paper bags, newspaper, construction paper (brown, yellow, black), rubber bands, white glue or tape

Make a copy of the Words to the Wise (**Reproducible 8B**) for each child. From brown construction paper cut two small triangles and one large triangle for each Words to the Wise Owl. (*The bases of the two small triangles should be the same width as the small ends of the bottoms of the paper bags. The bases of the large triangles should be the same width as the long sides of the bottoms of the paper bags.*)

Ask: Did your mom or dad or anyone else give you any good words of advice before you came here today? What did that person say? (*Invite the children to share. Share with them some of the good advice that you give to your own family if they have a hard time getting started.*) **Can you think of any other time when people have given you good advice?** (*Invite the children to share those words of wisdom.*)

Say: Jesus gave the people some good advice in today's Bible lesson. If the people followed this good advice they would be truly happy. All it took was for people to adjust their attitudes from thinking only of ME, ME, ME to thinking about others. This meant that sometimes the people had to completely change the way they previously had thought.

Continue: Today we are going to make a Words to the Wise Owl. On our owl we are going to attach some of the words of wisdom that Jesus gave to the people that day.

Have the children stuff the bags with the newspaper. Gather the ends of the bags and secure with rubber bands. Turn the bags upside down, so that the gathered parts are on the bottom. Glue the two small triangles and the large triangle on each bag as shown here. Cut two large circles for each bag from the yellow construction paper—these will be the eyes. Then let the children glue the Words to the Wise onto the bodies of their owls. Have the children set the owls in their rooms at home to remind them of what Jesus taught.

Sermon on the Mount

by LeeDell Stickler

> **Say:** Today we are going to be talking about one of Jesus' most famous teachings. We call it the Sermon on the Mount. Jesus talked to the people during this time about those things that were important for them to do and about how God wanted them to live.
>
> Give each of the children a sentence strip **(Reproducible 8B)** with one of Jesus' statements on it. Let some of the children have more than one if you have fewer than twelve children. Look in the biblical reference and pull out enough Scripture references so that each child will have a different one if you have more than twelve children. The children will form a teaching chorus. The children will form a Scripture wave (like a "wave" at a football game) at a designated signal, and will stand up and read their teachings, one right after the other.

Jesus went throughout Galilee teaching and proclaiming the good news of the kingdom of God. As he traveled he cured the sick and helped the people.

Scripture Wave

So Jesus' fame spread throughout all of Syria. The people, whenever they heard that Jesus was near, brought all their sick, and Jesus cured them all. He also taught them while they were in his presence.

Scripture Wave

Great crowds followed Jesus. When Jesus saw the crowds he went up the mountain to a spot where the people could see and hear him, and there he taught them what God wanted them to do.

Scripture Wave

The crowds were astounded at what he had to say. For Jesus taught not as a normal person but as one who had great authority.

Scripture Wave

Jesus went on his way down the mountainside and into the villages and towns. And everywhere he went he carried God's message to the people.

Scripture Wave

Fruitful Actions

Make a copy of the Fruitful Actions **(Reproducible 8C)** for each team of three children. Let the children cut apart the various fruit cards. If there is time the children may also color them or you may want to print them on colored paper instead.

Say: Jesus carried God's message with him wherever he went. God's kingdom was coming and in order to be a part of this kingdom, people had to live a certain way. One of the teachings for today talks about how good trees cannot produce bad fruit. This means that a truly good person will always try to live as God wants her or him to do and will do what is right.

Divide the children into teams of three. Have each team member decide who will be the tree, who will be the fruit placer, and who will tape.

Say: The object of this game is to hang only good fruit on the tree. We are going to place good fruit on the tree instead of picking good fruit from the tree. Each of the Fruitful Actions cards has a word or phrase on it. Read the word or phrase. If the phrase describes a good action, something we believe Jesus would want us to do, attach that piece of fruit to the tree. If the word or phrase names an action that we don't believe Jesus would want us to do, put that card in the rotten fruit pile. Let's see how many pieces of good fruit you can place on your tree. Let the taper yell, "Good Fruit!" when a team feels that it has attached all the good fruit it can place on its tree.

The child representing the tree will stand with arms outstretched. The fruit placer will attach the pieces of good fruit to the tree.

Sing and Celebrate

Sing together the song "Jesus, Jesus, Hear My Prayer" to the tune of "Twinkle, Twinkle, Little Star."

Jesus, Jesus, Hear My Prayer
(Tune: "Twinkle, Twinkle, Little Star")

Jesus, Jesus, hear my prayer.
Help me love and help me share.
You are Teacher, Healer, Friend.
I know your love never ends.
Jesus, Jesus, hear my prayer.
I'm so glad that you are there.

Words: LeeDell Stickler © 1997 Abingdon Press

85

Supplies

Words of Wisdom (Reproducible 8B); sheet, blanket, or blindfold

Scripture Scramble

Have the children form a circle and sit on the floor. Select one child to be "IT." Have IT come to the center of the circle and kneel on her or his knees. Cover IT with a sheet, blanket, or blindfold so that IT cannot see any of the other children.

Point to one of the children and have them begin to read their Words of Wisdom **(Reproducible 8B)**. IT will begin to crawl toward the sound of that person's voice. IT can ask the person to repeat the Scripture three times by saying: "Say what?" IT and the person who is reading will change places if IT is able to find that person.

Play until everyone has had a chance to be IT or until the children get bored. Point out to the children that Jesus taught the people how to be happy and how to live as God intended for them to live.

Jesus teaches us how to live.

Supplies

Bible

Growing Up Prayers

Have the children come to the floor and sit in a circle. Show the children the Bible.

Say: I want you to repeat one of Jesus' statements that you can remember from today's lesson as I pass the Bible around the circle.

Have the children join hands and form a prayer circle when the Bible has progressed all the way around the group.

Pray: Thank you, God, for Jesus, who came to teach us how to live. Help us to listen to his teachings and try to follow his example. Amen.

Jesus teaches us how to live.

A Tree and Its Fruit

Use your Bible to help you fill in the missing words.
Color the fruit as the basket tells you.

forgiven

good

you

hate

others

judge

apple

yell

love

puppies

No
(Red)
tree bears
bad fruit.
Luke 6:43

(Yellow)
your
enemies
Luke 6:27

Do not
(Purple)
and you
will not
be judged.
Luke 6:37

Forgive and
you will be
(Blue)
Luke 6:37

Do to
(Orange)
as you would
have them
do to you.
Luke 6:31

Do not judge others.

Love your enemies.

Let your light shine before others.

You cannot serve God and wealth.

Forgive and you will be forgiven.

Do to others as you would have them do to you.

A good tree cannot bear bad fruit.

Turn away from anger.

You will get back as much as you give.

Blessed are the peacemakers.

Give your gifts in secret.

God knows what you need.

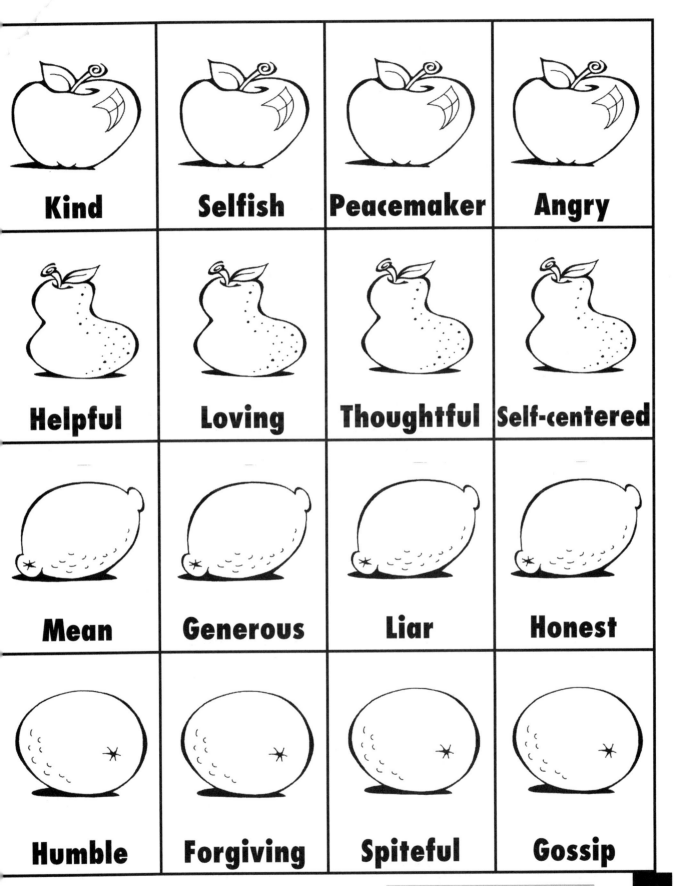

Kind	**Selfish**	**Peacemaker**	**Angry**
Helpful	**Loving**	**Thoughtful**	**Self-centered**
Mean	**Generous**	**Liar**	**Honest**
Humble	**Forgiving**	**Spiteful**	**Gossip**

Through the Roof

Bible Verse

Think of what Jesus went through. So do not let yourselves become discouraged and give up.

Hebrews 12:3, GNT, adapted

Bible Story

Mark 2:1-12; Luke 5:17-26

In the ancient Near East it was often thought that sin caused disease, especially those diseases that could not be cured. Because of this belief it was not unusual for people who had exhausted all normal channels for healing sickness to travel long distances to seek remedies from a holy man who was reputed to perform healing miracles.

Jesus already had a reputation for performing such miracles. So, crowds often gathered to see him when word got out that he was in a neighboring village. Four friends in today's story decide to carry their friend to see Jesus. The man in question was paralyzed and had exhausted all other avenues of healing. We see that their faith was strong, because they went to great lengths to see that their paralyzed friend met Jesus.

Some of the people who followed Jesus around, however, had other motives. Members of the religious establishment became more and more concerned about what Jesus was teaching as the number of Jesus' followers grew steadily. Perhaps they truly felt Jesus was teaching against the Law of Moses; perhaps they simply wanted to maintain peace in their communities and feared Jesus as a troublemaker. The healing of the paralyzed man created a problem, whatever the religious establishment's real motive was. Jesus forgave the man's sins—a blasphemy, since under the law of Moses, only God could forgive sins. By healing the man in this manner, Jesus claimed to have divine authority. What he did was considered a "blasphemous" act and drove a wedge between Jesus and the religious establishment. The crime of blasphemy was a crime against God punishable by death.

Jesus teaches us what God is like.

If time is limited, we recommend those activities that are noted in **boldface**. Depending on your time and the number of children, you may be able to include more activities.

ACTIVITY	TIME	SUPPLIES	
Mystery Message	**5 minutes**	**Reproducible 9A, crayons or felt-tip markers**	JOIN THE FUN
Don't Give Up!	10 minutes	electric fans, masking tape, two balloons, newspaper or cardboard tubes	
Cooperation	10 minutes	construction paper, yarn or ribbon, four cardboard boxes or four trash cans, scissors, tape, a penny or a metal washer	BIBLE STORY FUN
Bible Story: Your Sins Are Forgiven!	**10 minutes**	**None**	
Raise the Roof!	10 minutes	Reproducible 9B; construction paper; scissors; large piece of paper, or easel, or chalkboard; felt-tip marker or crayons	
Sing and Celebrate	10 minutes	None	
Hand Sign Prayer	**10 minutes**	**None**	LIVE THE FUN

Stories of Jesus - Elementary

Reproducible 9A, crayons or felt-tip markers

Mystery Message

Make a copy of the Mystery Message **(Reproducible 9A)** for each child in the group. Greet the children as they arrive.

Say: Jesus makes an unforgivable statement in today's Bible story. It is a statement that makes several people upset with him. But it is a statement that each of us is glad to hear.

Have the children color the specially marked spaces and uncover the mystery message: "Your sins are forgiven."

> **Jesus teaches us what God is like.**

Supplies

electric fans, masking tape, two balloons, newspaper or cardboard tubes

Don't Give Up!

Make a paper bat for each team. Fold several sheets of newspaper in half. Then roll the paper lengthwise. Tape the edges together. Or use a cardboard tube from a paper towel roll or from wrapping paper.

Divide the children into two teams. Have the children stand one behind the other in a line for each team. Use masking tape to create a starting line and a finish line *(about ten feet from the starting line)*. Set up the electric fan at the finish line and turn it on High. If you don't have access to electric fans, have a group of children act as the fans and blow the balloons away or fan them away with pieces of paper.

Say: The object of this game is to get the balloon across the finish line by batting it with the newspaper (or cardboard) tube *(on the ground, not in the air)*. **When you get to the finish line, you may pick up the balloon and run it back to the next person in line. The first team to have everyone get the balloon to the finish line wins the relay.**

When a team finally completes the relay **ask: What made this game so hard?** *(The fan was blowing the balloons away from the finish line.)* **Did you give up?** *(no)*

Say: In today's Bible story four friends set out to do a good deed for one of their friends who was unable to move. They wanted Jesus to heal their friend. But because of the crowds they couldn't even get close to Jesus when they got to the place where Jesus was teaching. However, they never gave up. In fact, they came up with a unique solution.

Cooperation

Supplies

construction paper, yarn or ribbon, four cardboard boxes or four trash cans, scissors, tape, a penny or a metal washer

Photocopy and cut apart the figure at the bottom of the page. Fold the figure along the dotted line. Tie a loop of yarn inside the fold so that the figure will hang from the loop. Tape a penny or a metal washer to the bottom of the figure to give it weight. You will need one figure for each team.

Cut a six-inch hole in a piece of construction paper. Tape this paper across the opening of a cardboard box or a medium-sized trash can. Make sure the paper is taped securely and pulled tightly across the opening. You will need one box or trash can for each team.

Cut the yarn or ribbon into two-yard lengths, one for each child. Give each child one length of yarn.

Divide the children into teams of three or four. Teams may consist of more members if you have a class of more than twelve children. Reduce the number of teams if you have a group with fewer than eight children.

Give each team a figure. Have each of the children thread his or her length of ribbon or yarn through the loop on the figure. Then tie the ends forming a loop. Each child should then place his or her loop over his or her head. Now all members of the team are linked to the figure character by their individual loops of yarn.

Place all the boxes and trash cans an equal distance from the starting line. Give the children space to maneuver around each box or trash can.

Say: In today's Bible story we hear about four friends who find a unique solution to a problem. Each team is going to reenact the story by carrying your injured friend (hold up the paper figure) **and lowering him through the hole in the roof** (point to the paper with the hole in it). **You will have to work together in order to get your friend inside the room. The only catch is that you cannot touch the figure with your hands in any way.**

Designate one box or trash can for each team. When you say "go" the teams will get to work carrying their friend to the house and lowering him through the roof.

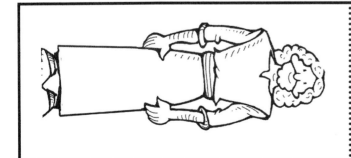 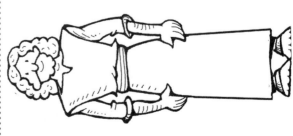

Your Sins Are Forgiven!

by LeeDell Stickler

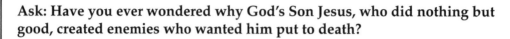

Ask: Have you ever wondered why God's Son Jesus, who did nothing but good, created enemies who wanted him put to death?

Say: The reason is that Jesus "rocked the boat." The things that Jesus said and did challenged what the people in Bible times believed was the right thing to do. The religious authorities actually thought that Jesus' behavior and Jesus' words encouraged people to break the laws of the day. That is why they didn't like Jesus and wanted to get rid of him. We see in this story an event that was wonderful to the person who was healed—an event that amazed all the people who saw it. The Pharisees, however, thought it was an act of blasphemy, because it did not fit their way of thinking. Blasphemy was a crime against God and it was punishable by death.

Teach the children the Response:

> Rock the boat, don't rock the boat Jesus!
> Rock the boat, don't rock the boat now.
> Rock the boat, don't rock the boat Jesus!
> Rock the boat, don't rock the boat now.

Have the children say this particular verse in a whisper, with their hands cupped to their mouths, leaning forward as if speaking in confidence.

Wherever Jesus went the people were sure to follow. They had heard about all the wonderful things Jesus did and said. Now they wanted to see and hear for themselves.

Response

One day Jesus went to visit some friends in the village of Capernaum. Word spread rapidly that he was in town. So people came from nearby villages and towns to see

him. In the crowd of people there were also a group of Pharisees and teachers of the Law. They, too, had heard about Jesus. They also wanted to learn more about what he had to say and what he did.

Response

There was a man in the town who could not move. He could not move an arm. He could not move a leg. He could not wiggle a finger or

ALL-IN-ONE BIBLE FUN

a toe. The doctors had not been able to make him well. So his friends decided to bring the man to Jesus.

Response

The man could not walk, so his friends carried his bed to the place where Jesus was staying. But by the time they got to the house, they found so many people already there that they could not get in. It was, in fact, so crowded that the friends could not even get close to Jesus.

How could Jesus heal their friend when they could not get close enough to speak to Jesus?

Response

Suddenly one of the men had an idea. "Let's go up to the roof. We can remove some of the tiles and lower our friend's bed through the hole. Jesus will have to see him then." And that is just what they did.

Carefully, the men removed the tiles. When the hole was just big enough for the man and his bed, the friends tied the ropes to the bed and lowered it into the room. Down, down, down went the man on his bed. When the pallet came to a stop, the man was hanging in the air, eye to eye with Jesus.

Response

Jesus looked at the man on the bed. "Friend," he said, "your sins are forgiven." All around the room, the Pharisees and the teachers of the Law gasped in horror. What had he said? How could he? How dare he? Only God could forgive sins!

Response

But Jesus turned to them and said, "Would it be easier for me to say 'Stand up and walk?' Either way you will know that I speak with the authority of God." Then Jesus turned back to the man on the bed. "Take up your bed and walk."

Response

The man stood up. Every part of his body moved just as it should. He rolled up his bed and went home, praising God. And everyone who saw what had happened was amazed and they praised God for giving Jesus the ability to do such wonderful things. But the Pharisees and teachers of the Law were not happy.

Response

Supplies

Reproducible 9B; construction paper; scissors; large piece of paper, easel, or chalkboard; felt-tip marker or crayons

Raise the Roof!

Make a copy of the Bible story picture **(Reproducible 9B)** for each team of children. *(You can have two, three, or four teams depending on the size of your class.)* Have each team cut a second piece of paper *(identical in size)* into sixteen squares. *(Fold the paper in half once, then again, then a third time, and finally a fourth time. Cut on the fold lines and you will have sixteen squares of approximately the same size.)* Have the teams put the story picture on the table in front of them. Cover the picture with the sixteen squares.

Say: We learn in the Bible that Jesus had a message to deliver to the people about God and what God is like. Today we are going to play a game to see if you can figure out the message. I will write a Bible verse on the chalkboard (or easel or a large piece of paper). I will write dashes instead of writing letters. Each team will have the opportunity to guess a letter. If the letter is in the word that team gets to remove one of the covering pieces. If that letter is found more than once in the verse, then the team removes a piece for each time the letter occurs. The object of the game is to uncover the picture.

Possible verses:
"Your sins are forgiven."
"Think of what Jesus went through."
"Stand up and walk."
"The people glorified God."

If you have additional time, make additional copies of the story picture, and let the children color it.

Supplies

None

Sing and Celebrate

Sing together the song "Take Up Your Bed and Walk" to the tune of "The Farmer In the Dell." Have the children do the suggested motions.

Take Up Your Bed and Walk
(Tune: "The Farmer In the Dell")

"Take up your bed and walk
Take up your bed and walk
Stomp your feet; then clap your hands,
Take up your bed and walk."

"Take up your bed and walk
Take up your bed and walk
Touch your toes; then turn around,
Take up your bed and walk."

"Take up your bed and walk
Take up your bed and walk
Swing your hips; then touch your nose,
Take up your bed and walk."

"Take up your bed and walk
Take up your bed and walk
Pat your head; then touch your knees,
Take up your bed and walk."

Words: Daphna Flegal

Hand Sign Prayer

Supplies

None

Bring the children together in the worship area. Teach the children signs from American Sign Language for the Bible verse litany.

Think—index finger faces the forehead and makes a small circle;
of—hook right index finger and thumb into the left index finger and thumb;
what—draw the tip of right index finger downward across the left open palm;
Jesus—place the tip of middle finger of the right open hand into the left palm and reverse;
went—hands with index finger extended are swung forward, one behind the other;
through—move right open hand forward between the index and middle fingers of the left hand which is facing you.

Say: It must have been hard for Jesus to have people like the Pharisees and the teachers become angry with him when he was trying to do something good for someone. Today in closing we will remember that Jesus didn't give up. We will remember how hard it was for Jesus to follow God's will whenever it's hard for us to follow. I will say a line of the prayer, and I want you to respond with the signs we just learned.

Pray: Dear God, from the very beginning people didn't understand what Jesus came to do ... *(Pause and sign.)* **When I try to do what's right and people make fun of me ...** *(Pause and sign.)* **When I work very hard and can't seem to make a difference ...** *(Pause and sign.)* **When people don't listen ...** *(Pause and sign.)* **We are glad Jesus didn't give up ...** *(Pause and sign.)* **Amen.**

97

Mystery Message

In today's story Jesus says a shocking thing!

Read Mark 2:1-12.

REPRODUCIBLE 9A

Color the spaces marked with a •

ALL-IN-ONE BIBLE FUN

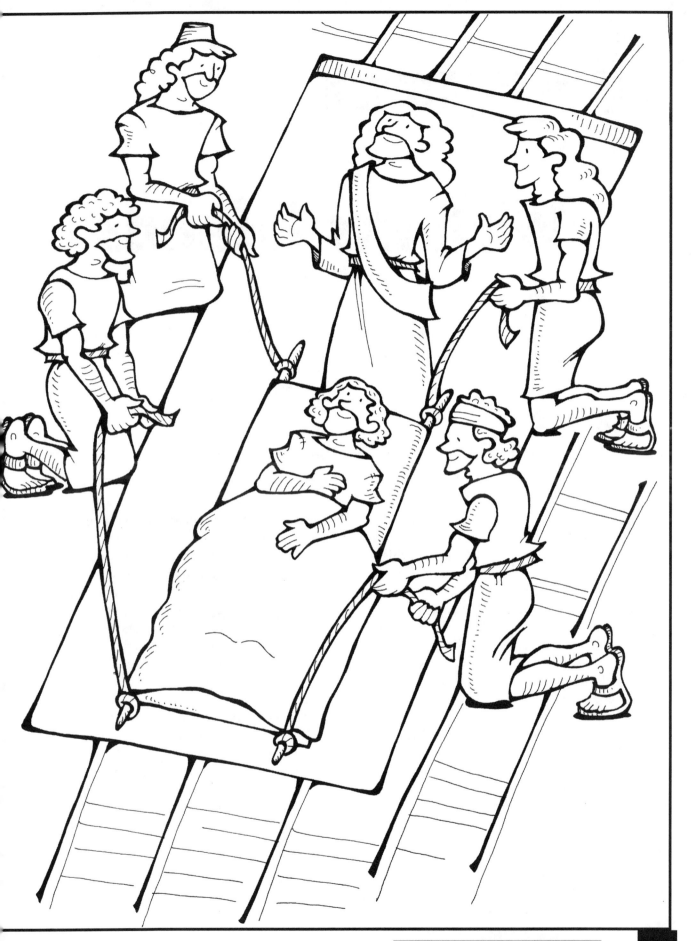

All-in-One

BIBLE ELEMENTARY

FUN

With His Friends

Bible Verse

The greatest love you can have for your friends is to give your life for them.

John 15:13, GNT

Bible Story

Luke 10:38-42; John 11:1-44

Jesus was born and grew up in a time of relative peace, but it was a Roman peace, enforced by Roman soldiers. With this peace also came a time of relative prosperity in almost every corner of the empire except Palestine. The people of Palestine were treated as little more than tax-paying units for extensive Roman building projects. There was much resentment among Palestinians because of this. Rumblings of revolt were just under the surface. But as long as life remained calm the Romans allowed the Palestinians to conduct their lives as they saw fit. The religious authorities tried to ensure that this was the case as much as possible. These leaders were always on the watch for signs of trouble, and to them, Jesus was trouble.

Today we hear about three people who were close friends with Jesus. Their names were Martha, Mary, and Lazarus—two sisters and a brother who lived in Bethany, a small village just outside of Jerusalem. Jesus often stayed with this family when he was going to Jerusalem. His last encounter with them came when Jesus raised his friend Lazarus from the dead. This act convinced so many Jews of Jesus' unique powers, says the Book of John, that the religious authorities decided to take steps to silence Jesus for good. Lazarus' raising led Jesus to the cross.

Children at this age are beginning to form friendships. They are learning what it means to be friends, even though their friends seem to change daily. But they are learning the basis of deep and lasting friendships. Hopefully, none of them will be asked to lay down their lives for a friend. As you look at today's story with your children, help them understand how much Jesus cared for his friends and how dear they were to him—dear enough to risk death.

Jesus loved and cared his friends.

If time is limited, we recommend those activities that are noted in **boldface**. Depending on your time and the number of children, you may be able to include more activities.

ACTIVITY	TIME	SUPPLIES	
Friendship Puzzle	**15 minutes**	**Reproducible 10A, watercolor felt-tip markers, scissors, envelopes**	JOIN THE FUN
Cheer Up, Friend!	10 minutes	shoe box, plain wrapping paper, tape, glue, stickers or old greeting cards, scissors, things to go in the box such as crayons, safety scissors, and a Friendship Puzzle (Reproducible 10A)	
Cross the River	10 minutes	masking tape, table, twelve small objects such as pencils, crayons, or small plastic blocks	BIBLE STORY FUN
Sing and Celebrate	10 minutes	None	
Bible Story: Mary, Martha, and Lazarus	**5 minutes**	**None**	
Lazarus, Come Out!	15 minutes	Reproducible 10B, scissors, cardboard tubes, crayons or felt-tip markers, yarn or ribbon, plastic ring six-pack holders	
Bible Verse Scramble	5 minutes	index cards, felt-tip marker, optional: CD player and CD of Christian music	LIVE THE FUN
Friendship Circle	**5 minutes**	**None**	

Stories of Jesus - Elementary

Supplies

Reproducible 10A, water-color felt-tip markers, scissors, envelopes

Friendship Puzzle

Make a copy of the the Friendship Puzzle Bible Verse **(Reproducible 10A)** for each child in the group. Greet the children as they arrive. Give each child a copy of the poster and watercolor markers.

Say: Today's Bible verse is about friendship—a special friendship. When we hear about Jesus and read the Bible we sometimes forget that Jesus was a real person with friends. Even though he traveled around a lot, he still had friends whom he cared about and loved. In today's Bible story Jesus goes to help three of his friends—Mary, Martha, and Lazarus. Because he helps them, many people believe that this was the event that caused the religious authorities to want to put Jesus to death.

Have the children use the watercolor markers to decorate their Bible verse poster. Encourage them use many colors so that they can create colorful posters.

Have the children cut the posters into eight to ten puzzle pieces when they have finished decorating them. Put the pieces into envelopes and put the envelopes in a basket or bag. Have each of the children draw an envelope out of the bag and reassemble the puzzle that someone else has created for them.

The class members may also choose to make puzzles for other persons. Make as many copies of the Bible verse poster as you feel will be needed. Once they have put together the first puzzle children may put the pieces back in the envelope and swap envelopes with another person.

Jesus loved and cared for his friends.

Cheer-Up, Friend!

Make a class Cheer-Up Box to give to a child from your church who is sick. Help the children cover a shoe box in plain paper. Wrap the lid separately. Let the children decorate the box by adding stickers or by gluing on pictures cut from old greeting cards.

Let the children help think of things to put in the box. You might share items that are already in your room like crayons, construction paper, a pair of safety scissors, and one of the Friendship Puzzles. Deliver the box to the child with a photocopy of today's story. If there is not a child who is sick in your congregation, design the box for an adult who needs cheering up. Change the contents to reflect the recipient.

Supplies

shoe box, plain wrapping paper, tape, glue, stickers or old greeting cards, scissors, things to go in the box such as crayons, safety scissors, and a Friendship Puzzle (Reproducible 10A)

Cross the River

Supplies

masking tape; table; twelve small objects such as pencils, crayons, or small plastic blocks

Bring the children together in an open area of the room. Divide them into teams of three. Mark the banks of the "river" with masking tape lines. The river should be about ten feet across. Designate a space for each team. Place a table on the other side of the river. On the table place the twelve small unbreakable objects (such as small plastic blocks, crayons, or pencils).

Say: Today's lesson is about Jesus' special friendship with three people. Something happened to one of those friends, and Jesus risked everything to go to them and help. We are going to play a game of rescue. Each team will represent a rescue unit during a flood. Two of you will start out as the boat. The third will be the Captain. It is up to the team to go across the flooded "river" (point to the space designated by the masking tape) **and rescue the children who are stranded there.**

Show the children how to make the boat: two players will grasp wrists and form a seat. The Captain will sit in this seat as the boat goes across the river and back.

Say: The boat will only hold one child at a time, so the teams must make as many rescue trips as they can in the time allotted. The persons on the team will change places after each rescue until everyone has had a chance to be the Captain.

The Captain will pick up one of the objects and hold it until the boat gets back to the team dock during each trip across the river. When all of the objects have been rescued the game will be over. The winner will be the team with the most rescued.

Sing and Celebrate

Supplies

None

Sing together the song "He Can Do a Miracle" to the tune of "If You're Happy and You Know It." Do the suggested movements, then let the children make up additional movements such as "bump a hip" (let two children bump their hips together).

He Can Do a Miracle
(Tune: "If You're Happy and You Know It")

Oh, Jesus is God's Son,
clap your hands. (clap, clap).
Oh, Jesus is God's Son,
clap your hands. (clap, clap).
He can do a miracle, 'cause
he's the Son of God.

Oh, Jesus is God's Son,
clap your hands. (clap, clap).

stomp your feet, shout hooray…

Words: Cynthia Gray, Linda Ray Miller, and Fran Porter © 2001 Cokesbury.

103

Mary, Martha, and Lazarus

by LeeDell Stickler

> Today's story is done as a reader's theater with several biblical characters involved. It does not require movement. Make a copy of the script for each child in the group. Highlight the part each has been assigned. Sit in a circle so that all the children can see one another and hear the dialog. Invite older children or youth to read the parts if you have mostly nonreaders in class. You will need these characters: Mary, Martha, Lazarus, Jesus, Messenger, Disciple #1, Disciple #2, Thomas, Crowd Member #1, Crowd Member #2, Pharisee, High Priest.

Martha: Mary, our brother is sick. We should send word to our friend Jesus. He will come make Lazarus well.

Messenger: Lord, your dear friend Lazarus is very ill.

Jesus: Lazarus will not die. But his illness will make it possible for me to show God's glory to the people. I cannot go there right now, but in two days we will leave.

Disciple # 1: Teacher, do you think that is a good idea? The last time we were in Jerusalem the people wanted to stone you.

Jesus: Our friend Lazarus has fallen asleep, but I will go and wake him up.

Disciple #2: But sleep is good. He will get well.

Jesus: I meant that Lazarus has died. We need to go to him. What you will see will surprise you.

Thomas: Then let's all go with you.

Martha: What took you so long to get here? Lazarus has been dead now for four days! But I know that even now God will give you what you ask for.

Jesus: Your brother will rise to life.

Martha: I know all about the resurrection on the last day.

Jesus: No, I am the resurrection and the life. Those who believe in

ALL-IN-ONE BIBLE FUN

me will never really die. Do you believe this?

Martha: I believe that you are the Messiah, the Son of God.

Mary: Lord, if you had just been here, our brother would not have died!

Mary and Martha: Come and see.

Crowd Member #1: See how much Jesus loved him. He is crying.

Crowd Member #2: He gave sight to a blind man, didn't he? Could he not have kept Lazarus from dying?

Jesus: Take the stone away!

Martha: Jesus, Lazarus has been dead for four days. It will smell bad.

Jesus: Didn't I tell you that you would see God's glory if you believed? Thank you, Father, that you listen to me. For the sake of these people here please raise our friend Lazarus. Lazarus, come out!

Lazarus: What is going on here?

Jesus: Unwrap him from his burial cloths.

Pharisee: What shall we do? Look at what this man has done. If we let this go on, then the Romans will destroy our Temple and our nation!

High Priest: It is better for one man to die than to have a whole nation destroyed.

Pharisee: What shall we do?

High Priest: Surely he will come to the Passover festival. Send word around that if anyone sees him they should tell us where he is. We will arrest him.

Ask: What wonderful thing did Jesus do for his friends? *(He raised Lazarus from the dead.)* **Why was it dangerous for him to come to his friends?** *(The people there wanted to stone him.)* **What happened after Jesus raised Lazarus?** *(The high priests decided that Jesus had to go.)* **When were they planning to arrest him?** *(When Jesus came to Jerusalem for the Passover.)*

Say: Jesus risked his life to help his friends, knowing what was going to happen. He also used this as an opportunity to show that people who were close to him just who he really was and help them understand.

Supplies

Reproducible 10B, scissors, cardboard tubes, crayons or felt-tip markers, yarn or ribbon, plastic ring drink six-pack holders

Lazarus, Come Out!

Make a copy of the cover for the Scripture Turbo Tube (**Reproducible 10B**) for each pair of children. Each child will make a Turbo Tube to take home, but two children can use one set to play with in class.

Have the children decorate the Scripture Turbo Tube cover in any fashion they choose. Glue or tape the cover onto the cardboard tube. Trim any excess paper that extends beyond either end.

Cut ribbon or string into twelve-foot lengths. Each child will need a length. Thread the two strings through the tube. Cut the six-pack holder rings apart to form three, two-loop handles. Tie a set of handles to the ends of each string.

Have the children work in pairs to play the game "Lazarus, Come Out!" Each player will hold onto the two handles and move away from the other player until the strings are tight. Slide the Scripture Turbo Tube to one end.

The player closest to the Turbo Tube will snap her or his hands apart and send the Turbo Tube to the other player, saying "Lazarus, come out!"

To receive the Turbo Tube players will keep their hands together. When the Turbo Tube gets to the receiving player that player will say, "I am the resurrection and the life." Then he or she will send the Turbo Tube back across the string or ribbon.

Say: Jesus proved to those who saw, without any doubt, that he was God's Son, the promised Messiah, when he raised his friend Lazarus from the dead. He also convinced the religious authorities that he was not a person who should be allowed to continue to go around the countryside stirring up trouble. The time had come and they had to do something about Jesus. Jesus risked it all when he came to help his friends. But he loved and cared about them, even if helping them meant giving up his life.

Jesus loved and cared for his friends.

106

Bible Verse Scramble

Supplies

index cards, felt-tip marker, optional: CD player and CD of Christian music

On index cards write the words to the Bible verse grouped in this fashion: "The," "greatest love," "you," "can," "have," "for your," "friends," "is," "to," "give," "your life," "for them." Break up the words more frequently if you have more than twelve children. Write the words in groups of two or more if you have fewer than twelve children. Adapt the game to fit your situation.

Bring the children together in an open area of the room. Give each child one of the cards. Make sure the cards are in a random order.

Say: Today we learned just what a great friend Jesus was. He was willing to sacrifice his life in order to help his friends Mary, Martha, and Lazarus. He was also able to show people that he really and truly was God's Son. Each of you has a card that is a part of the Bible verse. As I sing you will pass the cards to the right. When I stop singing, take the card you have and see if you can assemble yourselves in the order of the Bible verse for today.

Sing the words printed below to the tune of "God Is So Good." Repeat the verse as many times as needed for the activity. If you are uncomfortable singing in front of the children, play a CD of Christian music.

> The greatest love.
> The greatest love.
> The greatest love.
> Is to give your life.

Friendship Circle

Supplies

None

Have the children form a circle standing very close together. Have each child place his or her arms over the shoulder of the child on either side. This forms a very close circle.

Say: Today's Bible story showed us how much Jesus loved his friends. We love our friends as well. One of the things we can do to show love for our friends is to pray for them. We are going to "huddle" as they do on a football team. When I get to the end of the prayer I will say, "one, two, three!" Then we'll all shout "Amen" and break the huddle.

Pray: Dear God, we thank you for our friends. We are glad that Jesus, too, is our friend. Help us to love and care for our friends just as Jesus did. One, two, three, Amen!

The greatest love you can have for your friends is to give your life for them.

John 15:13, GNT

REPRODUCIBLE 10A

ALL-IN-ONE BIBLE FUN

I am the resurrection and the life.

I am the resurrection and the life.

All-in-One BIBLE FUN ELEMENTARY

Out of the Tomb

Bible Verse

For nothing will be impossible with God.

Luke 1:37

Bible Story

Matthew 27:32–28:10

Today's Bible story is both tragically sad and gloriously happy. It is the story of the crucifixion and resurrection of Jesus Christ—the most important story ever told, and the heart of Christianity itself.

The execution of Jesus as a criminal was a death that was long, painful, and extremely humiliating. It is a story about the lowest depths of being human, and that is what makes the story so powerful. This is the depth of suffering to which God was willing to go to save us from ourselves. God was willing to sacrifice Jesus, God's only Son, to bring us back into the right relationship with God. But without the crucifixion there would be no Easter.

According to the Book of Matthew several of the women watched from afar as their friend and teacher was put to death. They were also the ones who set out on the morning after the sabbath to anoint Jesus'

body in the Jewish tradition. And it was these women who first heard the wonderful news: "Jesus is alive!" Perhaps the women were more involved in these events because they were perceived as nonthreatening. They could move about and be seen in different places without being thought of as revolutionaries or troublemakers. But when they brought the news of Jesus' resurrection back to the other disciples, the great despair that had hung over the group changed to great elation.

Easter is the highlight of the Christian year. It is because of this day that we celebrate the birth of the baby in the stable. But it is harder to celebrate a cross than a baby. Help the children make the connection with the great gift that God gave to the people. Children may have questions about how all of this came about. Even as adults we do not know. But this we do know for certain: With God nothing is impossible.

God raised Jesus from the dead.

If time is limited, we recommend those activities that are noted in **boldface**. Depending on your time and the number of children, you may be able to include more activities.

ACTIVITY	TIME	SUPPLIES	
Butterfly Masks	**15 minutes**	**Reproducible 11A, construction paper, scissors, stapler and staples or tape, crayons or felt-tip marker**	JOIN THE FUN
City Search	10 minutes	doll or action figure to represent Jesus	BIBLE STORY FUN
Sing and Celebrate	5 minutes	None	
Bible Story: One Week in Jerusalem!	**10 minutes**	**Butterfly masks (Reproducible 11A)**	
Oh, Happy Day!	15 minutes	Reproducible 11B, scissors, black construction paper, wax paper, colored art tissue, white glue, shallow bowls or cups, paint brushes, newspaper, masking tape, optional: crayon shavings, iron	
Touch Happy and Sad	5 minutes	Reproducible 11B, construction paper, scissors, masking tape	LIVE THE FUN
Prayer Stack	**5 minutes**	**Reproducible 11B, scissors**	

JOIN THE FUN

Supplies

Reproducible 11A, construction paper, scissors, stapler and staples or tape, crayons or felt-tip markers

Butterfly Masks

Make a copy of the butterfly mask **(Reproducible 11A)** for each child in the group. Cut construction paper into one-inch by twelve-inch strips. Greet the children as they arrive.

Say: Today our Bible story tells about the saddest day and the happiest day. To celebrate the happiest day we are going to create butterfly masks. The butterfly has come to stand for the time when God raised Jesus from the dead. We all know that the butterfly begins life as a tiny egg, hatches out as a larva, becomes a caterpillar, spins a cocoon, and emerges as a totally different creature—a butterfly. We are going to "become" butterflies today to remind us that we become like new creatures who will never really die when we believe in Jesus as God's Son.

When the children have finished coloring their butterflies, let each cut out the "butterflies." Fit the construction paper strips to children's heads so that the masks will fit. An adult should cut around the eye holes so that they do not get too large or impair the vision of any of the children.

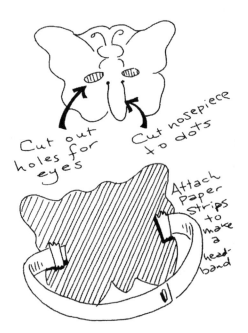

Cut out holes for eyes

Cut nosepiece to dots

Attach paper strips to make a headband

God raised Jesus from the dead.

112

City Search

Supplies

doll or action figure to represent Jesus

Bring the children together in the storytelling area.

Say: When Jesus and his friends came to Jerusalem to celebrate the Passover, the people welcomed Jesus with palm branches and shouts of "Hosanna!" Jesus' friends didn't know that there was a plot afoot to arrest Jesus and to kill him. But first the religious authorities had to find Jesus. They knew he was somewhere in the city, but they didn't know where. So they bribed one of Jesus' friends, Judas, to tell them where they could find him. It must have been hard to try to find one man in a city that was filled with Passover visitors before Judas agreed to help the authorities.

Say: Let's play a game. This doll (or figure) is going to represent Jesus somewhere in the city of Jerusalem. One of you will be the High Priest's guard. The others will be the people who know where Jesus is. You will shout "Hosanna!" when the guard is far away from Jesus, instead of shouting when the guard is near Jesus, to confuse the guard.

Select one child to be the High Priest's guard. Have the guard hide his or her eyes or step outside the room while you hide the doll or figure. Invite the guard to come back into the city and begin the search. The group will try to lead the guard away from where Jesus is staying as the guard slowly moves around the room. To do this the children will shout "Hosanna!" when the guard is far away, and stay silent when the guard close by.

When Jesus is discovered choose another guard; then hide the doll again.

Sing and Celebrate

Supplies

None

Bring the children together in the storytelling area.

Say: In the Book of Mark, after Jesus died and was placed in the tomb, three women went to the tomb to take care of Jesus' body. But when they got to the tomb, their sorrow turned to joy.

Sing together the song "Three Kind Friends" to the tune of "Three Blind Mice."

Three Kind Friends
(Tune: "Three Blind Mice")

Three kind friends,
Three kind friends,
Go to the tomb,
Go to the tomb,
They find the stone has been rolled away,

And Jesus is no longer there to stay.
He's alive on this first glad Easter day.
Oh, what great joy!
Oh, what great joy!

Words: Sharilyn S. Adair © 2001 Abingdon Press

113

One Week in Jerusalem!

by LeeDell Stickler

> **Say: Today's story is an action story, and we will build in the action. We will move from station to station, accumulating actions. We will move from station to station while doing the actions we have collected.**
>
> Set up eight stations in the room. There don't have to actually be eight separate stations, but move so that you go from one section to another, even if you return to the same place. If you don't have the space, walk around the table and pretend you are moving to another station.

Day 1

Station 1: Jesus and his friends came to Jerusalem to celebrate the Passover. All along the road people gathered. They had heard about this man and all that he said and did. They broke branches from the palm trees beside the road and waved them in the air, saying "Hosanna! He comes in the name of the Lord!" *(Hold hands overhead and wave back and forth, saying, "Hosanna! He comes in the name of the Lord!" as you walk to the second area.)*

Station 2: Jesus went up the mount to the Temple. There he planned to sit and teach the people. But what he found was not a place to pray but a marketplace with vendors and moneychangers. "Get out of my Father's house!"

he shouted as he overturned the tables. *(Stomp feet angrily and point while saying, "Get out of my Father's house!" Wave hands and shout, "Hosanna! He comes in the name of the Lord.")*

Station 3: Jesus' disciples went to the city gate. They were looking for a man carrying a water jar. This man had a house where Jesus and his followers could eat the Passover meal. There were many women with jars but no men. "Wait!" said one of the disciples. "There he is. Follow that man!" *(Pretend to hold a water jar on your shoulder and walk. Stomp and point saying, "Get out of my Father's house!" Hold hands overhead and wave, saying, "Hosanna! He comes in the name of the Lord.")*

114

Thursday

Station 4: Jesus sat at the table with his friends to eat the Passover meal. He passed around the wine and the bread. Then he told his friends, "Whenever you do this, remember me." Where was he going? *(Shrug shoulders and hold hands up questioningly. Pretend to hold water jar. Stomp and point saying, "Get out of my Father's house!" Hold hands overhead and wave, saying, "Hosanna! He comes in the name of the Lord.")*

Station 5:

After dinner Jesus went to the garden to pray. Jesus knew what was about to happen, and wanted God to guide him and be with him. But while he was there the soldiers came. They arrested Jesus and took him away. *(Hold hands behind back as though in chains. Shrug shoulders. Pretend to hold water jar. Stomp and point saying, "Get out of my Father's house!" Hold hands overhead and wave, saying, "Hosanna! He comes in the name of the Lord.")*

Station 6:

The council asked Jesus many questions. The soldiers made fun of him and beat him. Pilate, the Roman governor, couldn't find a problem with Jesus and washed his hands of the whole thing. *(Pretend to wash hands. Hold hands behind back. Shrug shoulders. Pretend to hold water jar. Stomp and point saying, "Get out of my Father's house!" Hold hands overhead and wave, saying, "Hosanna! He comes in the name of the Lord.")*

Good Friday

Station 7:

So Jesus was put to death on the cross. On either side of him were criminals. His friends gathered at the base of the hill. They cried for their friend Jesus. *(Pretend to cry. Wash hands. Hold hands behind back. Shrug shoulders. Pretend to hold water jar. Stomp and point saying, "Get out of my Father's house!" Hold hands overhead and wave, saying, "Hosanna! He comes in the name of the Lord.")*

Station 8:

Mary came to the tomb to prepare Jesus' body for the final burial at first light the day after the sabbath. But instead of finding Jesus she found an angel. "The one you are looking for is not here. He has been raised as he said he would be." *(Put on butterfly masks and dance around saying, "For nothing is impossible with God." Pretend to cry. Wash hands. Hold hands behind back. Shrug shoulders. Pretend to hold water jar. Stomp and point saying, "Get out of my Father's house!" Hold hands overhead and wave, saying, "Hosanna! He comes in the name of the Lord.")*

115

Oh, Happy Day!

Supplies

Reproducible
11B, scissors,
black con-
struction
paper,
wax paper,
colored art tis-
sue, white
glue, shallow
bowls or cups,
paint brushes,
newspaper,
masking tape,
optional:
crayon shav-
ings, iron

Make a copy of the cross pattern **(Reproducible 11B)** for each child. Cut away the butterfly and cross squares at the top and save them for another activity. Dilute white glue with water. Cover the tables with newspaper.

Provide a piece of black construction paper and wax paper for each child.

Say: Even though the cross is a symbol of the saddest day it is also a symbol of the happiest day, because Jesus' body is not there. We know that God raised Jesus from the dead.

God raised Jesus from the dead.

Say: We have new life because God raised Jesus from the dead.

Have the children trace the pattern of the cross onto the black construction paper. Cut out the cross, leaving a cross-shaped hole in the center of the paper. Cut the wax paper so that it will completely cover the cross-shaped hole.

Encourage the children to paint small bits of colored art tissue with the diluted white glue on top of the wax paper. *(Place the tissue paper on the wax paper. Then paint over it with the glue solution.)* Place the wax paper behind the cross-shaped opening and tape securely with masking tape.

The sunlight will shine through the colors of the cross when the picture is held up to a window.

Say: This will remind us what a happy day it was when God raised Jesus from the dead.

Option: Use pieces of shaved crayons and place between two sheets of wax paper. Place a warm iron over the wax paper and gently press. Then remove. Tape the double thickness of wax paper behind the cross-shaped opening.

Touch Happy and Sad

Cut apart the butterfly and cross symbols **(Reproducible 11B)**. Tape each symbol to a square of colored construction paper. Randomly place the squares on the floor around the room. Attach a loop of tape on the backs to keep the squares from slipping when the children step on them.

Say: In the story of Jesus' last week on earth there are some very happy times and some very sad times. Everyone should stand on the butterfly if the sentence tells about a happy time. Everyone should stand on the cross if the sentence tells about a sad time.

Use these statements:
"The people greeted Jesus with palm branches when he came to Jerusalem." *(H)*
"The Pharisees told Jesus to make the people be quiet." *(S)*
"Jesus and his friends ate the Passover meal together." *(H)*
"This was the last time they would be together." *(S)*
"Jesus went to the garden to talk to God."*(H)*
"Peter, James, and John fell asleep and didn't keep watch." *(S)*
"Guards came to the garden to arrest Jesus." *(S)*
"Jesus was sentenced to die on the cross." *(S)*
"Mary brought spices to anoint Jesus' body." *(S)*
"When Mary got to the tomb an angel was there instead of Jesus." *(H)*
"God had raised Jesus from the dead." *(H)*

Supplies

Reproducible 11B, construction paper, scissors, masking tape

Prayer Stack

Place one of the cross patterns **(Reproducible 11B)** on a table where all the children can gather around. Have the children form a prayer stack. The first child will put his or her right hand on the cross. The second child will put his or her right hand on top of that person's hand and so on until everyone's right hand is resting on the cross pattern.

Say: We believe that God raised Jesus from the dead. We believe that God gave Jesus new life, and because we believe in Jesus, God will give us new life as well.

Pray: Dear God, thank you for the gift of life. It fills our hearts with joy to know that because of Jesus, we will never really die. Amen.

Supplies

Reproducible 11B, scissors

> **God raised Jesus from the dead.**

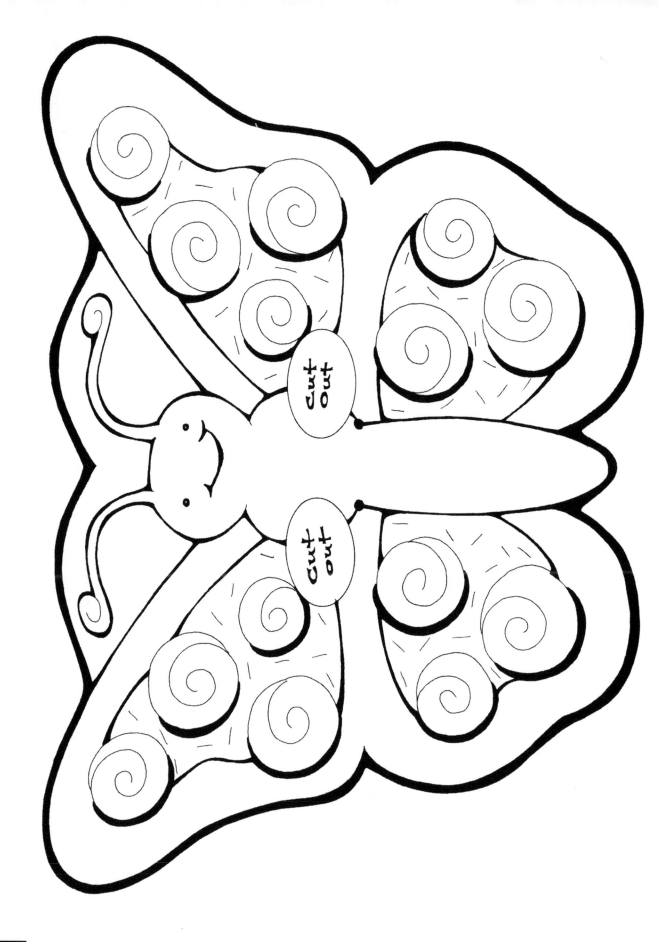

Cut out

Cut out

REPRODUCIBLE 11A

ALL-IN-ONE BIBLE FUN

On the Road

Bible Verse

The Lord has risen indeed.

Luke 24:34

Bible Story

Luke 24:13-35

On the road to Emmaus after Jesus' death occurred one of the most widely beloved events of the New Testament. The hopes of many of his followers died with Jesus when he died on the cross. For three years they had left everything to follow this charismatic teacher. Now he was gone, and there were confusing stories being passed around. The Romans were saying that someone had broken in and stolen Jesus' body. The women who were Jesus' followers were telling about an empty tomb and a meeting with an angel. No one knew quite what to believe. Obviously some did not believe what Jesus had told them about being crucified and rising again on the third day.

The two men who were traveling down the road to Emmaus had obviously not yet been able to figure out exactly what the events meant that surrounded Jesus' death. Though the rumors of crucifixion and even of resurrection were spreading, they had not had time to assimilate all of this information.

As they traveled they came across a man traveling alone and invited him to accompany them on their journey. The men did not recognize that this man was their risen Lord even when he taught them about the meaning of Scriptures. The implication is that it takes an openness to belief to recognize the risen Christ. It was only when Jesus broke bread with them that they knew who he was. Once they recognized Jesus as the risen Lord they knew that the signs had been there all along.

This is often the same with us. We are so busy looking for the meaning and purpose of our lives that we miss it until we allow ourselves to become open to it. We have to arrive at Emmaus before we understand that God has been on the journey with us all along.

Jesus lives!

If time is limited, we recommend those activities that are noted in **boldface**. Depending on your time and the number of children, you may be able to include more activities.

ACTIVITY	TIME	SUPPLIES	
On the Emmaus Road	10 minutes	**Reproducible 12A, pencils or crayons**	JOIN THE FUN
Pack It Up!	15 minutes	brown paper grocery bags; hats, sweatshirts, sweatpants, scarves, shoes	
Steppin' Out	10 minutes	Reproducible 12B, newspaper, tempera paint, fingerpaints or washable poster paint, paintbrushes, dishpan, water, paper towels, soap, optional: flip flops	BIBLE STORY FUN
Bible Story: Down the Emmaus Road	10 minutes	None	
Excuse Me, Please!	10 minutes	blindfold	
Sing and Celebrate	10 minutes	None	
Pillow Pass	10 minutes	Reproducible 12A, crayons or markers, tape or stapler and staples, newspaper, optional: CD player and CD of Christian music	LIVE THE FUN
Prayer Parade	5 minutes	None	

Supplies

Reproducible 12A, pencils or crayons

On the Emmaus Road

Make a copy of the word puzzle **(Reproducible 12A)** for each child in the group. This puzzle is easy enough for even nonreaders to do. Greet the children as they arrive.

Say: In today's Bible story two men meet a stranger on the road. This stranger is one big surprise to them when they finally figure out who it is. After this encounter it became very clear to them that a wonderful miracle had happened.

Show the children how to cross out the designated letters to reveal the mystery name. *(Jesus)* When the children finish working the puzzle, let them color the picture.

> ## Jesus lives!

Supplies

brown paper grocery bags; hats, sweat-shirts, sweat-pants, scarves, shoes

Pack It Up!

Say: Today's Bible story tells us about a special journey down the road from Jerusalem to Emmaus. But as soon as the men made it to their destination, they turned around and came back with excellent news. Jesus was alive! Let's pretend we are taking a journey. Like in Bible times we won't carry suitcases. People at that time carried all their belongings in baskets or bags. We will get to our destination, dress, undress, repack the bag, and return to our original starting place.

Divide the children into teams. You will need no more than four persons on a team, otherwise the game will get too long. Pack a brown paper grocery bag for each team of four. Use one of each of these items of clothing: hats, scarves, sweatshirts, sweatpants, shoes.

Give each team leader one of the bags. At the starting signal the first person on the team will carry the bag to the finish line; open it up; dump out the contents; put on all the clothing items; come back to the starting line; take off all the clothes; and put them in the bag for the second person in line. The game will continue until all members of each team have finished. If you have a small class let them work against time rather than each other.

Steppin' Out

Supplies

Reproducible 12B, newspaper, tempera paint, finger-paints or washable poster paint, paintbrushes, dishpan, water, paper towels, soap, optional: flip flops

Make a copy of the footprint poster base **(Reproducible 12B)** for each child in the group. Cover the floor with newspaper. Place dishpans of water and paper towels nearby. (You may need other adults to assist you with this activity.)

Say: Many of the roads that went from town to town were built by the Romans when Jesus lived on earth. These roads were built to last—surfaced with cut stones over a roadbed that was often a meter deep. These roads were known as the "ways" and were lifelines between the cities for both trade and security. The original roads were made so that the Roman armies could travel more easily, but they became much more than that. Travel about Palestine could be extremely dangerous in spite of Rome's efforts to rid the region of lawlessness. There were still many spots where bandits could lie in wait to attack unsuspecting pilgrims and traders. For this reason travel during this time period was not only dangerous, but uncomfortable. People traveled from city to city only when the trip was absolutely essential, and they never traveled alone.

Continue: We do not know exactly why the persons were traveling in our Bible story today. Perhaps they were returning to their village after the Passover. But this barefoot journey would change their lives and that of others forever. They discovered that Jesus was alive!

 | **Jesus lives!**

Have the children make a poster to take home and hang up in their room. They may work in teams of two. Let the children choose the colors they want for their footprints. Make sure they all remove socks and shoes. Have their partners paint the bottoms of their feet with thick tempera or other washable poster paint. Then let them step carefully onto their Bible verse posters.

Let the children wash their feet in the dishpan of water and dry them with the paper towels after printing their posters. If you don't wish to let them do this barefoot have one or two a pairs of flip flops for the children to use, paint the bottoms of the flip flops with the washable paint, and press the flip flop bottoms onto the posters. Run water over the bottoms of the flip flops to remove the paint. Blot dry with newspaper or paper towels.

Down the Emmaus Road

by LeeDell Stickler

Teach the children signs from American Sign Language for the phrase: "Jesus is alive." The children will use these signals as responses in the story several times. Practice the response until the children become familiar with it.

Jesus—Place the tip of your middle finger of the right open hand into your left palm and reverse.

is—Extend pinky finger. Move back and forth.

alive—Both "A" hands (hands in a fist) with your thumbs pointing up pass up the sides of your chest, beginning at the waist.

Engage the children in the story by letting them add the sound effects and body motions as indicated.

Two of Jesus' followers were on their way to a village named Emmaus on the same day that Jesus' tomb had been found empty. Emmaus was about seven miles from Jerusalem. (*Children stomp feet up and down in a walking motion.*)

As the men walked they talked about all that had been happening in Jerusalem. (*Say over and over: peas and carrots, peas and carrots.*)

Sign: Jesus is alive!

As they walked and talked Jesus himself drew near to them and began to walk along with them. The men saw Jesus but they didn't recognize him. (*Put hands over eyes.*)

"What are you talking about?" Jesus asked them, joining right in step. (*Stomp feet up and down as though walking.*)

ALL-IN-ONE BIBLE FUN

Sign: Jesus is alive.

"You must be the only person in the world who doesn't know what happened in Jerusalem these past few days. Have you been asleep?" (*Touch forehead with both hands then extend arms upward.*)

Jesus answered, "What things?" (*Shrug shoulders.*)

Sign: Jesus is alive.

"The things that happened to Jesus of Nazareth. He was crucified. We had such great hopes that he was the Messiah." (*Clasp hands in front of body in gesture of hope.*)

"Yes," said the other, "but the most remarkable thing happened this morning. Some of the women in our group went to the tomb. But they could not find his body. They came back telling us of angels who reported that Jesus was alive. When the men went to the tomb they didn't see Jesus or angels." (*Pretend to peer into the tomb.*)

Sign: Jesus is alive.

"How foolish you are! All this happened and still you are slow to believe. Did Jesus not tell you that he would be raised from the dead?"

And Jesus began to teach the men the Scriptures that told about himself. (*Shake finger.*)

Sign: Jesus is alive.

As the travelers got near the village of Emmaus, Jesus pretended that he was going further. But the men held him back. "Stay with us; the day is almost over and it is getting dark." (*Hold hands out in front to indicate "stop."*)

Jesus came in to eat with the men. He took the bread and said the blessing. Then he broke it and gave it to them. The men's eyes were opened! They recognized Jesus! But Jesus had disappeared from their sight. (*Put hands over eyes and then remove quickly.*)

Sign: Jesus is alive.

The men turned to each other. "Wasn't it like fire burning inside when he talked about the Scriptures?" So even though it was evening the two men jumped up and ran all the way back to the city. When they found the disciples they told them, "The Lord has risen indeed! We have seen him!" (*Stand up and run in place.*)

Sign: Jesus is alive.

BIBLE STORY FUN

Supplies

blindfold

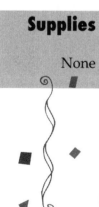

Excuse Me, Please!

Ask: Where were the men going when they met the stranger on the road? *(to Emmaus)* **What made the stranger angry?** *(when they still had problems believing in what Jesus had told them)* **When did the men recognize Jesus?** *(when he broke the bread at mealtime)* **What did they do then?** *(They rushed back to Jerusalem to tell the others.)* **Why didn't they recognize Jesus at first?** *(The Bible doesn't tell us.)*

Say: Perhaps they were not expecting to see Jesus, a man who had been dead and resurrected. Perhaps they were not very familiar with him and just didn't recognize him. The Bible leaves this as a mystery to us. Let's see if you can be more observant.

Have the children come together in the open area of the room. Select one child to be "IT." Put a blindfold on IT.

Say: Everyone will be able to move freely about the room until IT says "Stop!" Then everyone has to stop moving. IT will move about and try to find someone. Whenever IT touches someone he or she will say, "Excuse me, please. But who are you?" Then IT will try to discover who that person is by feeling his or her face and head. If IT makes a correct identification, that person will become the next IT, and the game will begin again.

Play until all the children have had a chance to be IT or until the children get bored. Make sure for safety's sake that there are no obstacles for IT to trip over while blindfolded.

Say: The men may not have recognized Jesus at first; but once they did they hurried back to Jerusalem to spread the good news. Jesus is alive!

Sing and Celebrate

Supplies

None

Sing together the song "Do You Know?" to the tune of "Do You Know the Muffin Man?" Sing the first verse as a question to the children. Have the children respond by singing the second verse.

Do You Know?
(Tune: "Do You Know the Muffin Man?")

Do you know he is alive,
Is alive, is alive?
Do you know he is alive?
Jesus is alive!

Yes, I know he is alive,
Is alive, is alive.
Yes, I know he is alive.
Jesus is alive!

Words: Daphna Flegal

126

Pillow Pass

Make a pillow from two copies of the Footprint Poster base **(Reproducible 12B)**.

Ask each child: Do you know Jesus lives?

Encourage the child to **respond: Yes, I know Jesus lives.**

Then have the child sign his or her name on either of the poster bases. Continue until all the children have the opportunity to add their names.

Stack the two bases together with the names facing out. Tape or staple three of the sides together. Stuff crumpled newspaper inside the pillow. Tape or staple the fourth side together.

Have the children stand in a circle. Hand the pillow to one of the children.

Say: I want you to pass the pillow around the circle as I sing. When I stop singing, the person who is holding the pillow will say the Bible verse for today: "The Lord has risen indeed" (Luke 24:34).

Before starting the game you might want to practice saying the Bible verse several times. Start and stop singing (Sing "Do You Know?" from page 126) often enough that all the children get the experience of saying the verse. If you are uncomfortable singing, play a Christian CD.

Prayer Parade

Say: Not every prayer has to be quiet and solemn. Sometimes prayers can be noisy and happy. A prayer thanking God that Jesus lives probably should be a prayer that is happy and joyful.

Have the children form a line, one behind the other. March forward four steps. Then stop and **say: Jesus lives, we thank you God.** Have the children march forward four steps and repeat. March forward four more steps. Stop and **say: Hallelujah! Hallelujah!** Have the children march forward four steps and repeat. March forward four more steps. Stop and **say: Jesus lives and we are glad!** Have the children march forward four more steps and repeat. March forward four more steps. Stop and **say: Amen. Amen. Amen. Amen.** Have the children march forward four steps and repeat. March forward four more steps, turn and give a high five to the child behind you; have that child march forward four steps and pass the high five down the line.

> Jesus lives!

Supplies

Reproducible 12A, crayons or markers, tape or stapler and staples, newspaper, optional: CD player and CD of Christian music

Supplies

None

127

On the Emmaus Road

Mark out all the Xs. Mark out all the Ks.
Mark out all the Qs. Mark out all the Zs.
Who did the disciples meet on the Emmaus Road?

X Q Z K X Z Q K Q
J X Q Z K X Z Q K
X Q Z K Q X Q Z K
Q X E Z Z X K Q X
K Q X K Q K Z Q X
Q X Z Q S K Q Z K
K Q X Z X Q K Z Q
Q Z X K Q Z U K Z
X Q Z Q K X Q Z K
Q Z X K Q K Z Z S

ALL-IN-ONE BIBLE FUN

Jesus lives!

All-in-One BIBLE FUN ELEMENTARY

With Us Always

Bible Verse

And remember, I am with you always, to the end of the age.

Matthew 28:20

Bible Story

Matthew 28:16-20; Mark 16:14-18; Luke 24:36-49; John 20:19-23

We can be sure that when an event is included in all four Gospels, it had great significance to the people who were recording the events surrounding Jesus' life and death. The risen Christ and his commission for the disciples to go into all the world to teach God's word is at the center of who and what we are as a church.

Jesus knew that it was time to ensure that his message spread. So he commissioned his disciples to carry on his work. They would go to all the world; they would make disciples; they would baptize; and they would teach with the knowledge that Jesus would be there with them, helping them all the way. This was a formidable task, even though the world as they knew it was considerably smaller than the one we now know. The one assurance the disciples had was that they would not be alone.

The world of the disciples was a hard and unforgiving place, and their task would not be an easy one. Up until this time most of the converts to Christ were Jewish—people who were very much like the disciples themselves. Jewish law encouraged separateness from Gentiles. How could they do what Jesus asked? They were willing in spirit but ill-equipped in so many other ways. But Jesus promised them a helper. This helper would empower them to tell Jesus' story. Jesus said, "Remember, I am with you always." That promise was kept.

The promise is no less true for us. If we will accept the challenge of living and teaching God's word we will not be alone—ever! All we have to do is open our hearts. The Holy Spirit is with us always.

Jesus will always be with us.

If time is limited, we recommend those activities that are noted in **boldface**. Depending on your time and the number of children, you may be able to include more activities.

ACTIVITY	TIME	SUPPLIES	
All About Jesus	**10 minutes**	**Reproducible 13A, pencils or crayons**	JOIN THE FUN
Me and My Shadow	5 minutes	None	
Bible Grand Slam	15 minutes	Reproducible 13B, construction paper, masking tape, newspaper, optional: blocks or buttons	BIBLE STORY FUN
Bible Story: Going to Galilee	**5 minutes**	**None**	
Bible Jump Up	10 minutes	None	
Limbo Lollapalooza	5 minutes	ribbon or yarn	LIVE THE FUN
Happy Prayers	**5 minutes**	**None**	

JOIN THE FUN

All About Jesus

Make a copy of the word find puzzle (**Reproducible 13A**) for each child in the class. Greet the children as they arrive.

Ask: How much do you know about Jesus?

Say: You have been going to Sunday school and reading the Bible. Just how many words can you find in this puzzle that tell something about Jesus? I have a word list I will share when you need a hint. One of the things we learn as we learn about Jesus is that Jesus will always be with us no matter where we are or what is happening.

Word list: *disciples, stable, kind, manger, Son of God, forgive, cross, rose, Good News, loves, angels, Emmaus, shepherds, teacher, wise men, sea, elders*

> ## Jesus will always be with us.

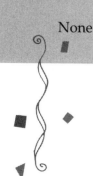

Me and My Shadow

Ask: What is the closest thing you can think of? (*Let the children make guesses.*) **What goes with you no matter where you go and does everything that you do? What disappears on a cloudy day but on a sunny day you can't get rid of it no matter how hard you try?** (*a shadow*)

Say: Today we are going to take turns being shadows. The reason is that in today's Bible story we learn that there is someone who promises to be close to us, even closer than a shadow, and he will be with us always.

Assign the children to be partners. One will be the mover and the other will be the shadow. It is the responsibility of the shadow to follow as closely as possible and do everything that the mover does. Let the shadow and the mover change roles after a minute or two.

Ask: How does it feel to have a shadow? How does it feel to be a shadow?

Say: We hear in today's story about the last thing Jesus told his friends to do and his last promise to them.

Bible Grand Slam

Supplies

Reproducible 13B, construction paper, masking tape, newspaper, optional: blocks or buttons

Make four copies of the Grand Slam Pictures **(Reproducible 13B)**. Make a score sheet. If you have a large class you may want to set up two games to keep things moving. It's more fun, however, when everyone is playing together.

Tape the Grand Slam Pictures **(Reproducible 13B)** onto pieces of construction paper. Then make a grid of construction paper on the floor, six pictures across and four pictures down. Arrange the pictures randomly in the grid. Designate a batter's box spaced about ten feet from the grid. Make a newspaper ball by loosely wadding up newspaper and surrounding it with masking tape. Do not pack it too tightly. Make a newspaper bat by folding several sheets of newspaper in half. Then roll the folded paper into a tube, taping the edges together.

Divide the children into baseball teams. Each team can decide on its name. Designate first, second, and third bases and home plate in the open area of the room. Somewhere between the picture grid and home plate set up a pitcher's box. Each team will decide on a batting order and who will pitch when they are in the outfield. There will be no need to have persons on bases on the outfield team. The outfielders can retrieve the newspaper ball or keep score.

The object of the game is for the batter to hit *(with the newspaper bat)* the newspaper ball so that it lands on one of the Grand Slam Pictures. The ball is considered "on" that square if it touches the colored square in any way. If the ball is touching two squares, the player can choose either one, or hit again.

The pictures will indicate the kind of hit the batter gets. *(If you don't physically have space for a baseball diamond, create one on paper and set the paper diamond on the table or floor. Let the children move a team of blocks or buttons to represent people.)* If a person hits the ball three times and the ball doesn't land anywhere on the grid, he or she strikes out. If the ball lands on a picture, then the team member *(with the help of the rest of the team, if necessary)* must provide certain information geared to that picture.

Manger: Tell something you know about Jesus.
Fish: Name one disciple of Jesus.
Cross: Name a book of the Bible that tells about Jesus.
Butterfly: Repeat a Bible verse.

Jesus will always be with us.

133

Going to Galilee

by LeeDell Stickler

Say: Today's Bible story recounts the story of Jesus' resurrection up until the time when he went to be with God. But Jesus left us with a promise. There will be parts for all of you as we tell the story.

The children say the rhythmic response in between each section of the story. The story will lead into the response by repeating, "And he will meet us there." The response will be performed by first having children hold hands out with palms up, wiggling their fingers and raising their arms above their heads. Then children's hands will come down and they will pat their knees alternately to indicate traveling. Vocally extend the word "We're" on the response (*much like "We're off to see the Wizard" from the song of that name from the* Wizard of Oz). Then on the first word, the children will slap their right knees with their right hands, then slap their left knees with their left hands, until the end of the response.

Response: **We're on our way to Galilee**
                    To Galilee, to Galilee.
                    We're on our way to Galilee,
                    To see the risen Lord.

Did you hear? Did you hear the news? The word is all over the city. Jesus, our friend and teacher, has risen from the dead! He told us in his own way that this would happen, over and over again—but somehow we just didn't believe. But now we know it's true! We've heard he's going on to Galilee, and he will meet us there.

Response:

We heard the story of the two Marys. Early on that sabbath morning before the town was even awake they went to the tomb. But there they found an angel instead of their friend Jesus. The angel said, "Jesus is going on to Galilee, and he will meet you there."

Response:

There was much concern when the guards of the tomb reported back to the high priests just what they had seen. The high priests thought and thought. "We can't let a story like this get around.

ALL-IN-ONE BIBLE FUN

Jesus is already so powerful. What if people heard about this? Instead, tell the people that Jesus' disciples crept into the garden and took the body away." But everyone knows what *really* happened. Jesus is alive and he is going on to Galilee, and he will meet us there.

Response:

We all came together to decide what we should do. Some of us had seen Jesus. Some of us had spoken to him. One of us had even touched him where he had been wounded by the soldiers. We know that Jesus is alive. Jesus is going on to Galilee, and he will meet us there.

Response:

So we hurried to the hillside in Galilee. And Jesus was there just as he had promised. Some of us fell down and worshiped him. Others who still doubted stood back a little. But then Jesus began to speak to us. "I want you to go to all people everywhere, and make them my disciples. Baptize them in God's name. And remember, even though I leave you today, I will be with you always, even until the end of the age."

Response:

Jesus made that promise on the hillside in Galilee. And he has kept it to this very day. He is with us no matter where we go or what we do. Even though he is no longer in Galilee—he no longer walks on the shore of the lake or on the streets of Palestine—Jesus is here just as he has always been. Jesus is with us always, now and forevermore.

Response:

Ask: Where did Jesus tell his friends to meet him? *(on a hillside in Galilee)* **What did he tell them to do?** *(Make disciples of all people.)* **What did he promise them?** *(to be with them always)*

Say: The job wasn't going to be easy, but Jesus promised to be with the disciples to help them. We know that living as disciples of Jesus today isn't always easy. But Jesus' promise to the disciples is a promise to us as well.

Supplies

None

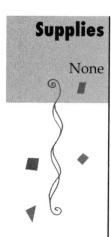

Bible Jump Up

Divide the children into teams of two. Have them pull chairs together so that they can discuss how they will respond.

Say: I am going to call out the names of people or things that have something to do with Jesus. *(The names are listed below.)* **Have someone on your team jump up if your team thinks it can tell me what the person or thing has to do with Jesus. The first team to have someone jump up gets to give its answer. If the answer is correct, that team gets a point. If the first team gives the wrong answer, the team with the next person to jump up gets to try. There will only be two tries per question.**

Use your own discretion as to whether an answer is correct. Listed below are the names and a brief synopsis.

Angels *(announced the birth, appeared to shepherds, told Mary and Joseph)*
Shepherds *(heard the angels, came to see Jesus, told others)*
Mary *(Jesus' mother; Joseph's wife or Mary at the tomb; Mary, sister of Lazarus)*
Joseph *(carpenter, Mary's husband)*
Wise Men *(followed the star, came to see Jesus, brought gifts)*
Star *(led the wise men to Jesus, stopped over the house, appeared in the sky)*
Elders *(at the Temple, talked with Jesus, amazed at his knowledge)*
Stable *(no room at the inn, where Jesus was born)*
Manger *(animal feed trough, Jesus' bed)*
Peter *(fisherman, followed Jesus, brother of Andrew)*
Andrew *(fisherman, brother of Peter, followed Jesus)*
James *(brother of John, fisherman, left father to follow Jesus)*
John *(brother of James, fisherman, left father to follow Jesus or Jesus' cousin, baptized Jesus, identified Jesus as God's Son)*
Dove *(symbol of Holy Spirit, alighted on Jesus after baptism)*
Synagogue *(where Jesus worshiped, read scroll, rejected by the people)*
Emmaus Road *(people met the risen Jesus and didn't recognize him)*
Tomb *(where Jesus was buried, empty, angel present)*
Lazarus *(raised from dead, brother of Mary and Martha, friend of Jesus)*
Martha *(sister of Lazarus, friend of Jesus)*
Pharisee *(didn't like Jesus and what he taught, tried to get Jesus into trouble)*

Add others if you have time. Play until time begins to run out or until the children become bored.

Jesus will always be with us.

Limbo Lollapalooza

Supplies

ribbon or yarn

Say: In today's story Jesus makes a promise to his disciples to be with them always. Jesus' promise also applies to us. In our class today we are going to think about all the places and times that Jesus is with us by having a Limbo Lollapalooza.

If your children are not familiar with the limbo give a small demonstration. Children will pass under a length or ribbon or yarn that is being held parallel to the floor. They will do this by leaning backwards and walking/hopping/scooting so that no parts of their bodies touch the ribbon or yarn as they move under it. Once everyone has been under the ribbon or yarn at a certain height, the ribbon or yarn will be lowered.

Select two children to hold the ribbon or yarn. They can take their turns at the end of the line. Or, you can tie the ribbon or yarn between two chairs if you have a small class. Have the children hold the ribbon or yarn at a reasonable height off the floor according to the sizes of your children. Have the children form a line. The first child will come forward, tell of a time or place when Jesus is with him or her *(at school, when sleeping, on the school bus, at soccer practice)*, and then limbo under the ribbon or yarn. That person will move to the end of the line. When all the children have been through one time, lower the ribbon or yarn and have the children limbo through again.

Say: There are many, many places and times when Jesus is with us. In fact, Jesus is with us all the time, in all places.

Happy Prayers

Supplies

None

Have the children stand close together in a circle.

Say: We are happy that Jesus is always with us. It keeps us from feeling alone. I am going to stretch out my hand into the center of our circle as we pray today. I want you to say thank you to God for something that makes you happy as each of you places your hands on top of mine. I will begin: "Thank you, God, for this wonderful class." *(Then let the children contribute. When everyone is touching hands, begin singing the Bible verse while walking around the circle several times. The Bible verse song is printed below and sung to the tune of "Are You Sleeping?")* **Amen.**

Bible Verse Song
(Tune: "Are You Sleeping?")

"And remember, and remember,"
Jesus said, Jesus said,
"I am with you always,

I am with you always
to the end, of the age."

Words: Daphna Flegal

137

All About Jesus

Find the words that tell about Jesus.

```
D I S C I P L E S Q
S T A B L E W L H Z
O F K I N D I D E X
N O E P Z Q S E P T
N O R M A N G E R H E
F G M N L O M S E A
G I A G O O E X R C
O V U E V D N Q D H
D E S L E N E W S E
C R O S S R O S E R
```

REPRODUCIBLE 13A

ALL-IN-ONE BIBLE FUN

Grand Slam Pictures

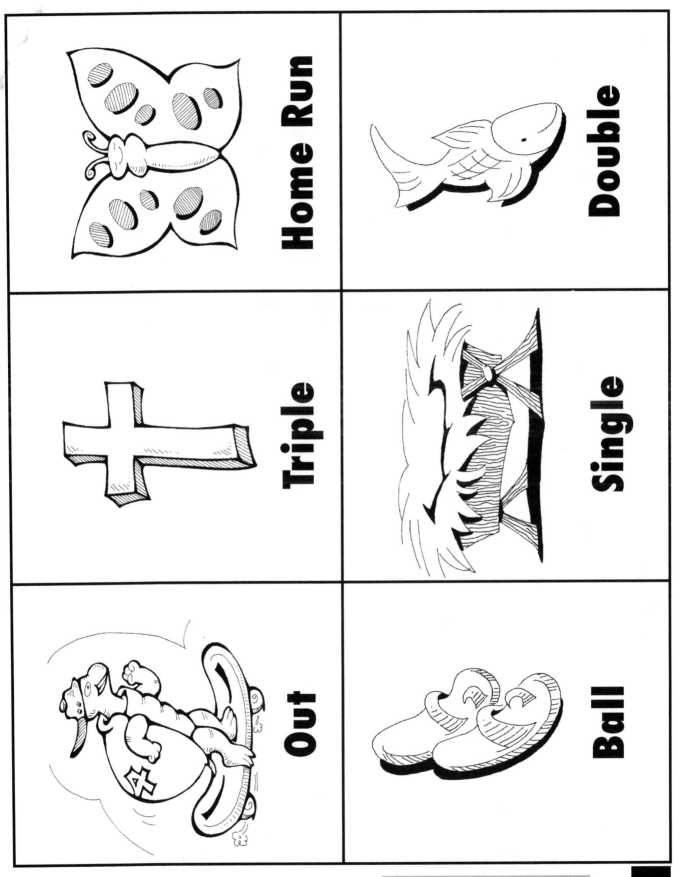

139

All-in-One

BIBLE FUN

Are you

- Feeling the budget pinch in your children's ministry?

- Unsure of the number of children you'll have in Sunday school each week?

- Working with a Sunday school program that doesn't meet each week?

LET THE FUN BEGIN

Order Today!

Preschool

Elementary

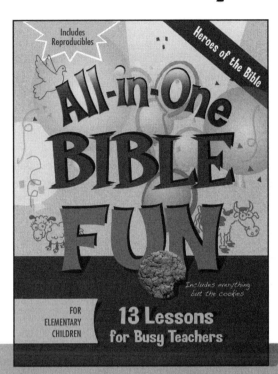

All-in-One Bible Fun

is available for preschool and elementary-age children. Each book will focus on a specific theme:

● *Stories of Jesus*

● *Favorite Bible Stories*

● *Fruits of the Spirit*

● *Heroes of the Bible*

• Thirteen complete lessons in each book

• No additional components to purchase

• Each book includes lesson plans with your choice of arrival activities, a Bible story, a Bible verse and prayer, and games and crafts

• Material is undated so teachers can use the books throughout the year

All-in-One Bible Fun: 13 Lessons for Busy Teachers

Stories of Jesus—Preschool 978-1-426-70778-0
Stories of Jesus—Elementary 978-1-426-70779-7

Favorite Bible Stories—Preschool 978-1-426-70783-4
Favorite Bible Stories—Elementary 978-1-426-70780-3

Fruits of the Spirit—Preschool 978-1-426-70785-8
Fruits of the Spirit—Elementary 978-1-426-70782-7

Heroes of the Bible—Preschool 978-1-426-70784-1
Heroes of the Bible—Elementary 978-1-426-70781-0

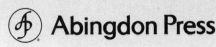 **Abingdon Press**

abingdonpress.com | 800-251-3320

One Room SUNDAY SCHOOL

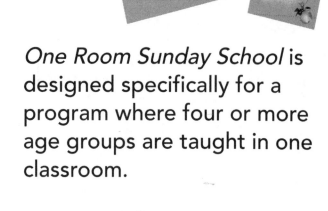

Working with a broader age group?

One Room Sunday School is designed specifically for a program where four or more age groups are taught in one classroom.

For children age 3 through middle school!

Students will grow together through comprehensive Bible study, application of Bible lessons to everyday discipleship, and a variety of age-appropriate activities.

 Abingdon Press